Rescued Pilgrim

R. H. FAGUNDO, MD

May your Journey take you
to the Fulfillment of God's
promised reward

R am Fagundo
Is 41 : 13

ISBN:978-1-7352383-0-2

In trying to put into words my life's story, I must confess I'm at a loss and I pray for the guidance of God through the Holy Spirit in accomplishing this task. Not only do I need God's help and inspiration to find the correct words, but I also pray that it may touch in some way the lives of those who may read it.

This "idea" of writing a book has been mentioned on several occasions by friends and fellow parishioners at St. Michael the Archangel Catholic Church, after reading some of the writings included here. It is through their encouragement, prayers, and insistence it finally materialized. For that, I am profoundly indebted and grateful, particularly to Ms. Patsy Shafchuk who made valuable suggestions and corrections to the "very rough" initial manuscript and to Mrs. Ethel DeMonaco and Mrs. Lee Ann Judd-Fagundo for their proofreading and editorial assistance.

But most importantly, I am most humbly thankful to my Almighty Father, God and Creator of all, for the undeserved gifts, inspirations and opportunities He has given me through my life, without which it would have been impossible to accomplish any of these. All the glory and honor be His, for I have only been the instrument which He deemed to use.

CONTENTS

Lord, open my eyes, that I may see You in everyone, in everything and everywhere, always.

Open my ears, that I may hear Your voice, and follow Your lead.

Open my mouth, that I may proclaim Your praise.

Open my mind, that I may grasp the immensity of Your love for me.

Open my heart, that in turn, I may love You always, and love only You.

Amen.

1   MY LIFE IN CUBA

My journey began in 1945 in rural Matanzas, Cuba, in a small town named Calimete. I am the first of three siblings born to the late Dolores Hernandez Santos and Ramon Fagundo Sanchez.

The intentions are not to relate a complete biographical account of my life but rather to highlight events and relevant facts that show how God's plan for my life has led me to the time of this writing.

I was born in a very small rural area in a town called Calimete next to the sugar mill that employed, in one way or another, almost everyone there. I was born at home, assisted by the local "comadrona" which is the equivalent of today's midwife (less formal education). My father and grandfather both worked at the mill, which was a seasonal job. My mother was a teacher's aide at the local school and after I was born, a full-time homemaker, taking care of the family that included her father-in-law, her husband, and eventually three children.

My father was a very smart man, whose dream in life was to become an architect. However, his father had quite a different opinion about studies and going to school in general. My father managed to finish the fourth grade after having run away from his house on two different occasions to attend a school near relatives in a nearby town. After the school year was over, he would return to his home to help his father laboring in the fields. He eventually learned a technical trade as "puntista"; that is a technician who converts the liquid sugar cane juice to its the granular form that we know as sugar. This became his lifelong job. He also designed and built his own house as well as houses for friends and relatives.

He was of strong and firm character, a strict disciplinarian yet very generous. He was an extremely good provider for the family despite his meager salary and limited opportunities. He was affectionate but rarely expressed it openly.

Because he could not realize his dream of getting the education of which he dreamed, he was insistent that his children obtain the best possible education and made immense sacrifices to this effect. This included moving the family to a bigger town to be close to better schools, while he would be traveling long distances to his job. He was always insistent on the importance of a good education as a way to succeed in life. He lived to see the results of his beliefs: a chemical engineer, an educator, and a physician.

When it was time for me to start secondary education, to assure I went to the best school, he moved the family to a bigger town that had a Catholic High School (Colegio Padre Felix Varela), in Colon, Matanzas.

Early in my parents' married life, due to the environment my father grew up in, he was not what you would call a believer or a religious person at all, although he did allow my mother to have us baptized, and receive First Communion. He even took us to Mass on Sundays occasionally, but did not go into church himself.

When I was about fifteen years old, I remember my parents getting married in the Catholic Church. He had only agreed to be married by civil law on their original wedding day. Since that time, on occasion, he would walk into church with us. This reminds me of the story of St. Monica and the conversion of her husband and her son St. Augustine.

My mother was truly a humble and meek person. She was soft-spoken, sweet, very generous and affectionate, and very devout to Our Lady and her son Jesus. I can recall seeing her on more than one occasion praying the rosary of which she was very fond.

Her formal education was to the eighth grade. She loved to read, especially about the lives of Saints, and their stories she told us many times as bedtime stories.

She carried the many crosses in her life, quietly and prayerfully, with great trust in our Lord Jesus Christ and Our Lady's intercession. She was always making sure that her faith was made known to us. I attribute my faith and devotion to her, and I always had that special bond with her beyond our closeness within the family.

I recall her telling me of her younger days living in the City of Matanzas, with her aunt and uncle after the death of her parents when she was going blind and specialists gave her no hope of recovering her sight. She was never told what the problem was, other than she was going to be blind. She told me that her aunt was a very devout person and told her to pray to St. Lucy, which she did constantly, and she attributed her recovery of sight to the Saint.

Few memories are still present of my early childhood, except those retold by my mother. I do remember being about 4 or 5 years old when a hurricane hit the town we lived in and how scared we all were. I remember looking out through cracks in the wooden wall of our house and seeing the storm-battered trees and debris flying everywhere. That is probably why I don't like stormy, windy days.

I also remember having a little goat that broke one of its back legs. I splinted it with two little boards tied with some pieces of rags and cared for it until it healed a few weeks later.

During my entire childhood up until about age thirteen or fourteen, I suffered from severe respiratory illnesses. These illnesses were eventually diagnosed as asthma which kept me out of school a great deal of time. It was my mother who stepped up to the plate to supplement the needed schooling and helped me stay on course, particularly during my earlier years.

I don't remember much about school in those early days, nor friends at school. I just spent many days at hospitals in Havana, where there was the only Pediatric Hospital close to us, about 110 miles away. There, an aunt would take me to the clinic or visited me when I was an in-patient at the hospital. Sometimes I would spend weeks in Havana. Perhaps this is a reason why I was always interested in being a doctor. I also recall the doctor in our town always parking his car in front of our house and me saying that one day I would be a doctor also. I worked hard and became the first in our entire family to graduate from college or to obtain a post-graduate education.

When it was time for me to go to Middle School, I went to Colon, Matanzas, about 15 miles from my hometown, to a private school. We traveled daily in a chartered car, a 1941 Ford, which the driver packed like sardines with all 14 of us students.

Another memory I have is when I was nine years old "operating" on birds my brother would catch for me with his "bird trap" or on chickens my father had. I would open them up using a Gillette double edge razor, look inside at the organs, then sew them back up with a needle and thread. The amazing thing was that they survived! I did this a couple of times until my father found out and that was the end of surgery for me for a while.

I remember at age eleven or twelve years old, my grandfather, while sitting on a chair with a towel around his neck in the back porch of the house, showing me how to shave him using a straight razor. That became "my job" until his death.

In my early teens, somehow the asthma seemed to be less severe and eventually went away spontaneously (probably a miracle in response to my mother's constant prayers) and I began to have a nearly normal teenage life. I began to have friends and participate in the normal kid's activities of sports which for a Cuban boy meant playing baseball and riding bikes. I truly loved it.

But this was too good to last! It was around the year 1958 and the political climate in Cuba was extremely tense for anyone not associated with the Batista regime which my father was not. Curfew was in place and everyone was afraid to talk to anyone.

On several occasions, my father was detained for interrogation by government officials but was lucky enough to be released to his family. We were not allowed to be outside much, much less talk with other kids. This had a lasting psychological effect on me. I never really had the opportunity to develop a close and lasting relationship in my early life, first because of illness and later due to the political climate of repression and retaliation.

Soon after Castro took over in Cuba, in January of 1959, my father, who had been a strong supporter of the Cuban revolution and Castro while he was hiding in the hills of the Oriente province, came home from a meeting and told my mother "we are in big trouble now, this guy is a communist". The rest of his family did not believe him and even stopped talking to him altogether.

The following year, on his trip to New York City, Castro made clear to the world who he was. How did my father know he was a communist? He never told anyone, just that he knew it, long before it was openly declared. But by then, it was too late for many.

I had managed to get a few close friends by this time, however, one of them was killed by the Castro militia in mid-1960; another was imprisoned in late 1960 and was serving 30 years after being betrayed by another friend; two friends had left the country and I never heard from them; another friend was fighting against Castro with a guerilla group in the mountainous regions of southern Matanzas, close to the Bay of Pigs. This friend I visited twice, taking him supplies and ammo as well as money from the sales of "revolutionary bonds" in our school. His parents lived across from us and were friends of my family. Just before I left Cuba, this last friend was caught along with 10 others and all were publicly executed. This was extremely hard on me.

I was just over 16 years old then and resolved not to be taken alive if caught in these activities because I knew the fate that awaited those caught. Of course, my parents were completely blind to this fact and my activities.

To make matters worse, in every city block of every city, there were "neighborhood watchdog committees" whose only mission was to spy on anyone not associated with the communist party. They would follow them every step taken out of their houses and had the authority to interrogate anyone they wanted to and even place them under arrest as they saw fit.

The way it worked was, as soon as you stepped out of your house, they would stop you and ask you where were you going and the reason why and for how long were you going to be out. Once they had this information, they would notify other committees on your route and your final destination, to corroborate your claim. If, for any reason, you deviated from your original plans, that would be cause for you to be put in jail and further interrogated by detectives (the so-called G2), as suspected contra revolutionary.

At this point, my father, after being interrogated and detained several times and our house searched once, decided to leave Cuba with the whole family. He made several attempts to take us out of Cuba via chartered boats from Varadero Beach where we went under the pretext of vacationing.

The Lord was certainly looking after us because in one of those attempts, the boat that was to pick us up was gunned down by government patrol boats. After this attempt, my father desisted and planned on getting us out through the Canadian embassy. However, after the Bay of Pigs fiasco, getting passports to leave Cuba was difficult and a step the government looked at unfavorably, especially in the more rural areas of the country.

After a lengthy wait and a multitude of hurdles and obstacles, it was finally time for us to legally leave our homeland. But you did not leave Castro's Cuba that easily! At the very last moment, government officials decided that my father couldn't leave the country until he had trained someone to do his job, knowing well that it would take time to do so.

My parents then made the most heroic, difficult, and selfless decision any parent could make. That is, to let go of their three minor children, send them to an unknown land alone so that they might have a chance for a better future in a free country; to set them free to fly from the repressive communist regime so they could have liberty and religious freedom, but uncertain of ever seeing them again.

No one was expecting us in Miami and we didn't know anyone either. We didn't know the language or the way of life here and didn't have resources for support.

Once we got to the airport terminal in Varadero, Cuban customs officials decided that we couldn't take all three suitcases. I thought it would be alright to take my clothes out of mine and place them in my brother's but was abruptly stopped and I was told to "just pick two suitcases", so mine   stayed   behind.

2   ARRIVAL TO THE USA

I don't recall much about the short flight to Miami other than I said some prayers and for the most part, kept my eyes closed. After all, we were told and believed, this separation was going to be for just a short time. I do remember boarding a Pan Am airplane and after take-off, there was a lot of cheering by the passengers.

We arrived at MIA at about two or three o'clock in the afternoon and were placed in a large room full of strange people and those that came with us on the flight. Slowly, the room began to empty until there were but a few of us left. At one point, I was taken by myself to a different room where suited men, seated behind a large desk, began to ask me questions over and over in a non-native Spanish accent. I remember feeling intimidated and threatened. It was obvious they didn't like my answers because they insisted that I was wrong and did their best to convince me that I was mistaken in what I thought I saw.

Most of the questions asked were about soviet missiles, which I happened to have seen in big semi-trucks parked on the roadways of my hometown, Colon, on their way to Cienfuegos. We came to the USA on August 25, 1962, shortly before the October 1962 missile crisis. All legal flights to and from Cuba were then suspended.

After what seemed like many long hours at the Immigration office and interrogation by those men, I was again reunited with my scared brother and sister and we then were placed in a van and taken for a long ride to a place called Camp Matecumbe, located near the Homestead Air Force Base. My brother and I were dropped at a small chalet type cabin where a person was waiting for us.

The van continued with my sister toward Florida City but we didn't know where she had been taken at the time. It was over two months later I finally got to see her again.

Camp Matecumbe and Florida City, among other places, were part of Operation Pedro Pan, run by the Catholic Welfare Bureau and The Archdiocese of Miami, with the late Monsignor Bryan Walsh being the spearhead of the program. This program eventually managed to help over 14,000 unaccompanied children from Cuba, with histories very similar to ours.

The above-mentioned person was waiting for us at the front cabin, which was a cozy and welcoming chalet. It was the office of the camp and not the actual lodging. He led us for about a third of a mile through swampy terrain among pine trees, using his flashlight, until we arrived at a clearing. Our accommodations consisted of five large army canvas tents filled with bunk beds three rows high, and the floors were made out of wooden pallets. There were metal lockers that served as dividers for the different grades within each tent and a single large light bulb in the middle of the tent. My brother and I were sent to different tents according to our school level and age group.

We arrived at the camp past 10 o'clock that night. We were tired, hungry, scared and most of all extremely lonely and I was just "numb", so sleeping that night was not a problem for me. It was probably the only night in many, many, many months in which I fell asleep without running out of tears. I remember that every night at bedtime, after prayers and turning the light off, they used to play a record of "The Platters" to help us fall asleep but also so that the crying and sobbing of the kids was not heard.

The following morning reality set in...shockingly. There were close to 600 kids in the camp, just like us. The camp itself was amid the everglades, full of pine trees along with rattle and coral snakes, raccoons, bobcats, swampy terrain, the occasional gator, and mosquitoes galore. There were few dry areas, only on the dirt road that led to the office and around the fixed wooden structures. After taking but a few steps outside those areas, your footprint would fill with water almost immediately.

Initially, there were only three wooden structures besides the tents that housed the kitchen and dining area, the infirmary, and one building for six bathrooms and twelve showers for the entire camp. There were two public phones, not always in working conditions.

Since this had been at one time a Boy Scout camp or retreat camp, there was a swimming pool!

Classes were being held at different pine trees, according to school grades. These classes were taught by school teachers and by the La Salle Brothers on open areas around the pine trees, which were marked with the different school grades.

Mass was celebrated every Sunday in a tent/chapel.

Eating was in two "shifts" according to grades, so even though my brother was in the same place, our contact was somewhat limited, usually at breaks, before dinner, and just before bedtime and on weekends. The dining area was in one of the buildings with seven rows of eight picnic tables each row, next to the kitchen.

Upon arrival at the camp, every kid received three pairs of white socks, three white t-shirts and underwear, a pair of blue jeans, and a pair of sneakers. When it was time to leave the camp, you were given a pair of dress pants and a shirt, dress shoes and a suit when going to college.

Making friends was relatively easy since everyone had a common denominator: being away from their parents and homeland. However, disappointments were also easy and I was already leery of getting too close to anyone for fear of experiencing the loss of another person. Psychologically speaking, I must have thought that if I didn't get close to anyone, I wouldn't get hurt anymore.

And it happened that every so often kids were sent out of the camp either to family members, foster homes, orphanages ("boys and girls houses"), or on college scholarships all over the country and you would lose contact with them. After graduating from High School, I was sent along with three other boys to the University of St. Thomas in Houston, Texas. Three of us became physicians.

The High School I graduated from, along with sixteen other students, Matecumbe High School, is a very special one, having only one graduating class, the class of 1963. It came to be by special circumstances. We all were to be graduating in Cuba after fulfilling all required curricula, however, now in the USA, we lacked the language requirements, American literature, and American history to be able to graduate here.

By special dispensation from the Board of Education, Monsignor Walsh created Matecumbe High School with the sole purpose of fulfilling the requirements we needed for graduation. The High School was to be dissolved afterward and all other students would go through the regular school system.

What is remarkable about this High School I think, is not only that it had only one graduating class, but that of seventeen graduates, there are four medical doctors, several engineers, lawyers, and successful businessmen. This, is quite remarkable in itself, not to mention the fact that we were in a foreign land. But that land was and still is, so far, the land of opportunity, of freedom and religious liberty, just as our parents had dreamed it would be.

After moving to Houston, I lost contact with my siblings for a couple of years until I found out that my brother was in Wilmington, Delaware, and my sister in Indianapolis, Indiana. After many inquiries, many pleadings, and visits to the welfare office, through a social worker, I was able to bring my brother with me to Houston. They would not allow me to bring my sister then. When my parents finally came from Cuba in 1966, they relocated to Houston, and my sister was then allowed to join us.

My first experiences in College were not flattering or encouraging at all. I still remember the first day at one of my classes in which every student was to introduce himself to the class, state where he was from and what were their aspirations in life. When it was my turn, I was so nervous I could hardly speak and when I finally did, few understood because of my poorly spoken English. When I said I wanted to be a doctor, many started to laugh. It was not a good day for me.

At the dorms, we were separated for us to learn the language faster, however, that turned out badly. My roommate had a dislike toward Mexicans, "wetbacks", as he called them and he assumed I was one. He rarely spoke to me and grudgingly returned the casual greetings. Never during the entire year did we had any sort of conversation.

After the school year was over, which I thought was a scholarship until I began to receive government notices for payment, we had to move out of the dorms for the summer. Three of us got an efficiency apartment for one person but all three lived in it. Then the search for work started. The fourth student's parents had arrived from Cuba and he moved with them.

I recall during these times, our meals consisting of "homemade pizza" which was toasted bread bought at a day old bread store, topped with catsup from packages from fast-food restaurants and grated cheese, also from fast-food restaurants, then put in the oven for a few minutes and voila, we enjoyed the pizza. Sometimes we were invited for dinner when visiting families and this we appreciated.

After many weeks of unsuccessful searching for a job, on our last day in Houston while saying goodbyes to friends, Providence again intervened. The manager of the apartment of the friend we were visiting overheard us and came over and offered us a job at an aluminum window factory. We started work the following day!

Shortly after this, the parents of one of the three arrived from Cuba and he left, so only another boy and myself remained in that efficiency apartment. We then had to get transportation since the car we were using belonged to the person who left. But getting our transportation was easier said than done. We could not get financing for $250; there were no cosigners. Thanks for public transportation!

Back in the '60s in Houston, Texas, being Black or Hispanic was not easy on public transportation. You had to board the bus through the rear door, and if you gave your seat to an old lady who happened to be Black, you were asked to exit the bus, again through the rear door. I never understood that.

When it was time to enroll in school again, I decided to go to the University of Houston, a State University, more affordable to me. I enrolled full time and kept my full-time job as well.

Working in that factory was a very tough job. There was a high turnover of employees because of the poor working conditions (no A/C, no heat), a very physically demanding job with a pay barely at minimum wages, starting at a dollar an hour.

After much saving, I bought a used car, so I felt very relieved about transportation.

One afternoon, while going to visit a Cuban family, I was stopped behind a car making a left turn when a Big Mack truck ran over my car, making it a twisted roll of steel. People who witnessed the accident said no one could have survived it. I only remember blessing myself with the sign of the cross and saying a Hail Mary prayer. The accident happened in the outskirts of Houston, in a scarcely built area, next to a railroad where extensive road construction was in progress.

The fire department found me sitting on some railroad tracks about two blocks away. I did not walk there. Nobody saw me get out of the car and walk there. I don't know how I got to the tracks but I was there and not in the car where I was at the time of the accident. There were cars in front and behind me and nobody saw me getting out of the car. I call this another miracle in my life. What else can it be?

I do remember the fire department taking me to Ben Taub General Hospital, which was the hospital for trauma victims at that time, and after many tests and x-rays, I was sent home with multiple broken ribs and blood in the urine which eventually cleared up in a matter of days.

Because of the limitation of broken ribs, I couldn't continue in that factory and so I had to get another job. I was hired as an orderly at St. Joseph Hospital during the night shift, and continued college in the daytime. They were very nice to me, allowing me to take naps after all the work was done and I could study in between jobs. I worked there for over a year. I remember enjoying the job, especially on weekends, when I spent most of the time in the emergency department where a certain physician was on duty. In busy times and on certain patients he would call me and let me suture, and I did so with eagerness.

By this time my friend and I had rented a two bedrooms apartment and my brother had finally joined me and was going to school. I then began training to be a draftsman and landed a good-paying job at an engineering company, Brown and Root Company, while still attending college. The money was good and the perks were excellent. They even suggested I switch to engineering and work for them when finished with school. Since I was a pre-med student then with sights set on medical school, I declined that offer.

While at this company, I recall working on a project with high-security measures in place. Later on, we found out the project was for NASA.

While attending the University of Houston, I befriended a Mexican American guy who was the lab assistant in one of my classes. He also wanted to go to medical school and that's how we connected. He was a mentor in many ways.

He graduated with a 4. 0 GPA and was just an outstanding person. He had applied to all medical schools in Texas and was turned down by all of them. I'm sure it was not due to lack of scholastic achievements, but rather, he had no money and he was a Mexican descendant with very dark skin and after all, that was Texas in the sixties.

Most medical schools demanded an upfront $2000 deposit for lab fees and equipment not including tuition, lodging, books, etc. He calculated it would cost him about $20,000 for that first year, that at a time when most salaries started at $1.25/hr. Needless to say, he was devastated. He became a lab technician instead and later we lost contact.

With all this knowledge now, I understand the reaction of the students on that first day of classes at the University of St. Thomas. But my desires to become a doctor were still very strong and my prayers intensified the more. I remember stopping at St. Anne Catholic Church on Westheimer Road in Houston many times a week praying for guidance and for a way to fulfill my dreams.

One afternoon, while at the foreign student's club at UH, I started to talk to this person who was speaking in Spanish with another student. We became friends and with time we exchanged our aspirations, frustrations, and life's experiences, etc. When he found out I wanted to go to medical school, he told me about the University of Costa Rica's Medical School and told me I should go there. He told me that his father oversaw the Costa Rican consulate in Houston and he would get me the necessary student visa. And so, he did. The Lord does work in mysterious ways indeed.

3   Journey to Costa Rica

I contacted the University of Costa Rica for information and details and soon my plans were underway. By this time, our family had been reunited in Houston, my father was working, and both my brother and sister attending school. My mother was also working, cleaning an office building next to our apartment, after hours, and we three kids used to help her.

I decided to finish college in Costa Rica on their advice, since that way I would have a better chance to be admitted to medical school. The school only admitted five foreign students and gave preference to those attending there; and so, this happened.

During my first year in Costa Rica, taking courses in humanities to complement what I had already taken, I had times of profound recollection and spiritual insights and composed many poems, writing them in a notebook. This notebook has been lost, however, a few of the poems survived, thanks to my mother who saved all those poems I sent her. It seems obvious to me now that I must have had a great faith and spirituality at the time, when considering the events during that year and my writings.

The poem that follows was written while waiting for a class on the balcony of the second floor in the building of Humanities and Social Studies. I just scribbled it down as fast as it came. This was usually the pattern in which these poems came to be. I will write them, first in the original version in Spanish, then the translated one. I'll use the same format for poems written in Costa Rica.

3.1 Mi Dios. Poema

MI Dios

Mirar al azul del cielo

Desde este balcón ruidoso

Es sentirse orgulloso

De tener lo que más quiero.

Bajar la mirada y ver,

Ver el polvo que se mueve,

Es pensar que todo muere

Que muere todo al nacer.

Más si alrededor miramos

Vemos al hombre y su obra,

Vemos el color que cobra

Todo lo que pensamos.

La vida, el hombre, su obra,

Es todo perecedero,

Sólo vive el que implora.

A Él, a quien más quiero.

San José, Costa Rica. Agosto 10,1967

3.2 MY GOD. POEM
My God

Looking at the blue of the sky

From this noisy balcony

It's to be proud

Of having what I most love.

Looking down and seeing,

Seeing the moving dust,

Is to think that everything dies,

That everything dies at birth.

And if we look around,

We see man and his works,

We see the color it takes

Everything we think about.

Life, man, his work,

It's all perishable,

Only lives he who implores

Him, whom I love most.

San José, Costa Rica. August 10, 1967

Soon after that poem, came a couple of others, later that same day.

3.3 INQUIETUD. POEMA
Inquietud

Inquietud…

Inquietud es todo aquello

Que Martí, Bolívar y Darío

Y otros tantos más sintieron,

Es poder decir

¡Te quiero!

Es lo que mueve al guerrero,

Es hacer un acto bello.

No es más que el propio ser

Saliéndose de sí mismo,

Buscando nuevos senderos

Por los cuales se ha de ir.

Inquietud…

Inquietud es la palanca que impulsa

El mundo donde vivimos,

Es la miel con que se endulza

Eso extraño que sentimos,

Propio de la juventud.

Es algo conmovedor

Que al ciego hace ver,

Es poesía, Es Amor,

Es algo más que comer.

Inquietud…

Inquietud es el pensar,

El pensar sobre la vida.

¿Y la vida?,

¡La vida es toda Inquietud!

Agosto 10, 1967

3.4 RESTLESSNESS. POEM
Restlessness

Restlessness…

Restlessness is everything

That Marti, Bolivar and Dario

And many others like them felt,

It is to be able to say

RESCUED PILGRIM

I love you!

It is what moves a warrior,

It is to do a kind deed.

It is nothing else but our being

Coming out from within,

In search of new ways

To express itself in.

Restlessness…

Restlessness is the lever that moves

The world in which we live,

It's the honey which sweetens

That strange feeling

Proper of our youth.

It's something moving,

That, which gives sight to the blind.

It is poetry, it is rhyme,

It is something more than time.

Restlessness…

Restlessness is to think,

To think about life,

And life?

Life is all restlessness.

San José, Costa Rica. August 10, 1967

3.5 JUVENTUD. POEMA
Juventud

Juventud…

Juventud…

Juventud que te añoro

Decía un pobre anciano

Recostado a su bastón,

Si pudiera otra vez verte,

Si contigo andar pudiera,

Qué feliz tú me harías,

¡Cuántas cosas yo hiciera!

Tú le das el color verde

A la tierra que me llama,

Eres carbón encendido,

Eres el fresco rocío,

RESCUED PILGRIM

Eres el candente amor,

Eres… Oh Juventud.

De bienes, nada me falta,

Por desgracia de todo tengo,

Tengo yo lo que no quiero,

Quiero lo que no tengo.

Yo te ofrezco mis riquezas

A cambio de tu dinero;

Siendo pobre tu eres rico,

Yo rico, soy el más pobre.

Más como volver no puedo

¡A ti, Oh que desgracia!

No quiero que a ti te ocurra

Lo que de tiempo me pasa.

No te excedas en abusos

Del verde que estás vistiendo,

No malgastes esa llama

Que arde dentro de tu pecho.

En los momentos de fuego,

Acuérdate del rocío,

Que después de ardiente sol

Humedece al hierberío.

Y del Amor,

El amor no lo conoces.

Tú luces tu traje verde

Y esperas a que anochece,

Para gastar de tu llama

Que poco a poco perece.

Juventud…

Si tuvieras mi experiencia

Qué gran bien te causaría,

Mucho más tú ahorrarías

De todo eso que tienes.

El verde de tu color

En gran árbol tornarías,

Belleza y esplendor

RESCUED PILGRIM

AL mundo tú le darías.

El fuego de tú corazón

Mucho no lo gastarías

Creo yo., lo guardarías

Para mejor ocasión.

El amor lo emplearías

En otras cosas mejores,

Ayudar a los peores,

En repartir tús alegrías.

Te diré yo del rocío

Y así llegar hasta el fin,

Qué si tienes un jardín,

Sin él es jardín vacío.

Y así terminó aquel viejo

Llorando ya de tristeza,

Con bastón y brazos caídos,

Inclinando su cabeza.

Un murmullo pude oír

Allá en la lejanía,

Eran las voces del viejo,

Del viejo que ya gemía.

Me acerqué y allí estaba,

Estaba en agonía.

Mi oído yo acercaba

Mientras el viejo decía,

Juventud,

Juventud de hoy,

Juventud verde, prenda querida,

Decirte adiós nunca puedo,

Sólo te digo, Hasta luego,

Hasta luego vida mía.

San José, Costa Rica. Agosto 10, 1967

3.6 YOUTH. POEM
Youth

Youth...

Youth...

Youth I Miss You,

RESCUED PILGRIM

Said a poor old man

Leaning on his cane.

If I could see you again,

If I could walk with you,

How happy you would make me,

How many things I would do!

You give the color green

To the land that calls me,

You are coal aflame,

You are the fresh dew,

You are the burning love,

You are, Oh Youth.

Of goods, I am not lacking,

Sadly, I have everything.

I have what I don't want,

I want what I don't have.

I'll give you all my riches

In exchange for your money;

Being poor you're rich,

RESCUED PILGRIM

I'm rich yet I'm the poorest.

And since I can never return

To you, Oh what sadness!

I don't want it to happen to you.

What happened to me in time.

Don't overdo in the abuse

Of the green you're wearing.

Don't waste that flame.

That burns in your chest.

In the moments of fire,

Remember the dew,

That after blazing sun

Wets the soil.

And Love...

You don't know love.

You look at your green suit

And you wait for night to last

To spend your flame

That gradually perishes.

Youth...

If you had my experience

How great a good it would do you.

Much more you would save

All that stuff you've got.

The green of your color

In great tree, you would become,

And beauty and splendor

You would give to the world.

The fire of your heart

You wouldn't spend so much

I think you, you'd keep it.

For a better occasion.

Love you would employ

In other better things,

Helping the worst,

In handing out joys.

I'll tell you about the dew

And so, go to the end,

That if you have a garden,

Without it, it is an empty one.

And so, ended the old man

Crying already of sadness,

With cane and fallen arms,

Tilting his head.

A murmur I could hear

Back in the distance,

They were the voices of the old man,

Of the old man who was already moaning.

I approached and there he was,

He was in agony.

To hear, my ear drew near

While the old man was saying,

Youth

Today's Youth,

Green Youth, dear garment,

I can never say goodbye to you,

I'm just telling you, See you later,

Until then my life, my love.

San José, Costa Rica. August 10, 1967

Being of Cuban ancestry and still a Cuban citizen at the time, I did think a lot about my homeland and its history. I was also very fond of the Cuban poet and patriot, Jose Marti and as a tribute to both, my birthplace and Marti I wrote several poems:

3.7   ALLÁ EN LA LEJANÍA. POEMA
Alla en la Lejanía

Allá en la lejanía

Donde el sol es más caliente

Existe la tiranía

De la maldita serpiente.

A lo lejos, allá. a lo lejos,

Donde un día fui feliz

Vive un pueblo sin reflejos

Porque ahora todo es gris.

Sólo tiene lamentos, llanto y tristeza

El pueblo noble y hambriento

Que sufre con rebeldía

La muerte que están viviendo.

Con ella están sufriendo

Todos los que la amamos,

Los de afuera, los de adentro,

Los que nos sentimos cubanos.

Y si sola te sintieras

Escuchad esta razón,

Aunque por ti morir tuviera,

Cuba, tú tienes mi corazón.

San José, Costa Rica. Agosto 15, 1967

3.8 THERE, IN A FAR DISTANT PLACE. POEM
There, in a far distant place

There, in the distance

Where the sun is hotter

Exists the tyranny

Of the malicious snake.

In the distance, there, in the distance,

Where one day I was happy

Live a village without reflections

Because now everything is gray.

There is only lamenting, crying and sadness.

The noble and hungry people

That suffers rebelliously

The death they're living.

With her are suffering

All of us who love her,

The ones from outside, the insiders as well.

All of us that feel as Cuban.

And if you would feel abandoned

Listen to this reason,

Although for you I would have to die

Cuba, you have my heart!

San José, Costa Rica. August 15, 1967

3.9 **LAMENTO CUBANO. POEMA**
Lamento Cubano

¡Oh! Cuánto necesitamos

De un Maceo y de un Martí,

RESCUED PILGRIM

De valientes de Bayamo.

De canciones de mambí.

Para nuestros abuelos

Aquello lució un sueño,

Murieron por nuestro suelo,

No dejaron tender dueño.

Lograron la Independencia,

A sangre y fuego ganaron,

Ganaron con vehemencia

La causa porque lucharon.

Los niños también lucharon

Porque sus padres lo hacían,

Los de adentro se quedaron,

Los de afuera ya irían.

Nada es fácil, ni ha sido,

Nunca fue ni lo será,

Con los bravos se ha obtenido

De Cuba la libertad.

Ellos tuvieron unión

Y un ideal más que fijo,

Fueron a la revolución,

Abuelo, padre e hijo.

Nunca fue más bello el sol,

Nunca más grande su gloria,

Cuando valientes guerreros

Obtuvieron la victoria.

Necesitamos del sol

Tan radiante y tan ardiente,

Necesitamos también

Hombres de sangre caliente.

Cuánto necesitamos

De Cuba, de amor, de Dios,

De volver a lo que amamos,

¡De decir, exilio adiós!

Oh Cuánto necesitamos

De un Maceo y de un Martí,

De valientes de Bayamo,

De canciones de mambí.

De jóvenes de antaño,

De los hombres del futuro,

De armas de hierro y estaño,

De ideales maduros.

¡Oh cuánto lo necesitamos!

San José, Costa Rica. Septiembre 14, 1967

3.10 A CUBAN LAMENTATION. POEM
A Cuban Lamentation

Oh, how much we have need,

Of a Maceo and a Marti,

Of the brave men from Bayamo

And the songs of the mambi.

To our ancestors,

That was like a dream,

To fight for liberation,

To die for us to be free.

They won our independence,

RESCUED PILGRIM

With blood and fire, they fought,

They sang a victory cadence,

Of victory or death, they thought only.

The children also fought

Because their parents were,

Those inside stayed,

Those outside joined too.

Nothing worthy in life is easy

Nothing will ever be,

But the brave had obtained

For Cuba, its liberty.

They were all in unity

And they had a single goal,

They went to the revolution

Grandfather, father, and son.

The sun was never so bright,

Nor so grand the glory,

As when at the end of the fight,

RESCUED PILGRIM

They have won the victory.

We all need of the sun

So warm and radiant,

But we also need men

That are brave and valiant.

How much we need

Our God, Cuba, of love,

To return to our roots,

To say, exile, farewell.

Oh, how much we have need,

Of a Maceo and a Marti,

Of the brave men from Bayamo,

And the tunes of the mambi,

Of yesterday's youngsters

And tomorrow's men,

Of weapons of steel and lead,

Of clear ideals.

Oh, how much we need it!

San José, Costa Rica. September 14, 1967

There was a hiatus in writing due to being busy working to have enough funds for the following school year, however, the writings returned with the return to school. The poem that follows was written on the birthday anniversary of Jose Marti. Here it is:

3.11 HOMENAJE. POEMA
Homenaje

Un veinte y ocho de Enero

En la Habana española,

Nació un cubano sincero

En una vieja casona.

Mil ochocientos cincuenta y tres

Ese mismo fue el año

En que una madre arrullaba

Envuelto en un pobre paño

Al héroe que ya soñaba.

Érase allá en la Habana

Donde todo era fogoso,

Donde más cruel la tirana,

Hacía sufrir a un mozo.

RESCUED PILGRIM

Desde muy joven sufrió

Los azotes noche y día.

Pero con ellos crecía.

Su valor, su poesía.

Para los niños fue un templo

Todo lleno de amor,

Y les dejó el buen ejemplo

De morir por el honor.

Al incrédulo, dió fe,

Al cobarde, dió coraje,

Por el mundo siempre fue

Predicando su mensaje.

Con honor siempre decía

Al monte guerrero vamos,

Vamos todos a pelear,

Es nuestro deber salvar

La Cuba de los cubanos.

RESCUED PILGRIM

Admiro del gran apóstol

No tan sólo su hombría,

Admiro su noble causa,

Admiro su poesía.

Estuvo en el destierro

Como ahora lo estamos,

Luchó como león fiero

Por lo mismo que amamos.

Habló y unió al pueblo ardiente

Disperso en la lejanía,

Murió allá en Oriente,

Dió todo lo que tenía.

Ese hombre tan ardiente

A quien hoy menciono aquí,

Aquel que murió en Oriente,

Ese fue José Martí.

San José, Costa Rica. Enero 28, 1968

3.12 HOMAGE. POEM
Homage

On the twenty-eighth of January

In Spanish Havana,

A sincere Cuban was born

In an old Spanish house.

Eighteen hundred and fifty-three

That was the very year

In which a mother cooed

Wrapped in a poor cloth

The hero who already was dreaming.

It was there, in Havana

Where it was all fiery,

Where the cruel tyrant,

Made the young man suffer.

From his youth he suffered

The scourging blows, night and day.

But with them grew,

RESCUED PILGRIM

His valor, his poetry.

For the children he was a temple

All filled with love,

And he set a good example for them.

To die for honor.

To the incredulous he gave faith,

To the coward, courage,

To the world, he was always going

Preaching the same message.

With honor he always said

To the mountains, warriors go,

Let's all fight!

It is our duty to save

The Cuban's Cuba.

I admire of the great apostle

Not only his manhood,

I admire his noble cause,

I admire his poetry too.

He was in exile.

As we now are,

He fought like a fierce lion

For the same reason we love.

He spoke and united the fiery people

Scattered in the distance,

He died there in Oriente,

He gave everything he had.

That faithful man

That today I mentioned here,

The one who died in Oriente

That was José Martí.

San José, Costa Rica. January 28, 1968

There were many other poems but the only ones that remain are the ones I had sent to my mother. She kept them and gave them to me once I came back. One such poem is this one that occurred to me while studying for final exams, before entering medical school. Here is the poem:

3.13 EL ÁNGEL DEL AMOR. POEMA
El Ángel del Amor

Estando solo una noche

Del cielo, un Ángel vi,

Y entre luces celestiales

Un coche,

Descendiendo hacia mí.

Detúvose aquel carruaje

A mis pies, muy junto a mí,

Y el Ángel en su lenguaje

A mis oídos dijo así:

"No te extrañes pobre hombre

Del porqué heme aquí,

Si yo he venido a ti

Es para que no te asombres.

Soy el Ángel del Amor,

Mensajero de Dios Padre.

Vengo a calmar el dolor,

Vengo a perdonar los culpables.

He venido desde lejos

Predicando mi mensaje

Y a todos los hombres dejo

Parte de mi equipaje.

Tomad,

Abrid bien tu mente,

Abrid más tu corazón,

Mantente siempre ferviente,

Escuchad esta razón:

El niño Jesús vendrá

Muy pronto ya de María

Y quiero que en Navidad

Reine la paz, la armonía.

El los vendrá a salvar

Del dolor, de la agonía,

Y fuerzas les dará cada día

Al descender al altar.

RESCUED PILGRIM

Yo les vengo a enseñar

Lo que de Él he aprendido.

He aprendido a amar

A todos sin distinción,

Pobre o rico, es igual,

Sea de América o Europa,

De África, China o Japón

Pues ante El todos son,

Hijos que siempre ha de amar.

Sí,

Sé muy bien que sois humano

Y es por eso que te digo,

Que ames siempre a tu hermano

Y también al enemigo,

Aunque él no te quiera a ti.

Adiós, es tiempo ya de partir

Pues mi destino es muy lejos,

Pero antes te he de decir

Tan sólo un simple consejo.

Si sólo te sintieras

Y buscaras una luz,

Búscalo a Él, quién más te quiera,

Pues murió por ti en la cruz.

Aún en el esplendor

E inmóvil como estaba,

Vi marcharse al que me hablaba,

El Ángel del Amor.

San José, Costa Rica. Mayo 5, 1968

3.14 THE ANGEL OF LOVE. POEM
The Angel of Love

One lonely night,

A long time ago,

Coming down from Heaven

An Angel I saw,

And among celestial lights,

A beautiful carriage

Swiftly approached.

The carriage stopped

RESCUED PILGRIM

Just at my feet,

And the Angel in his language

At me whispered so:

"Don't wonder poor soul

Of why am I here,

If I have come near

It's not for you to ponder."

"I am the Angel of Love,

Messenger of God the Father.

I have come to heal the pains,

I have come to pardon sinners"

"I come from a distant place,

Proclaiming the same message,

And for all men's grace,

To each I give a passage"

"Take it,

Open your mind,

Open even more your heart,

Always keep your faith,

Listen to what I say"

"The babe Jesus will come

Very soon, from mother Mary,

And I want for this one time,

Peace on earth to always reign"

"He will be the Deliverer

From all pains and agony,

And each day He will strengthen you

By His presence on the Altar"

"I have come to show you all

What from Him I have learned.

I have learned to love at any cost,

Whether rich or poor or foe or friend,

Or black or white or red or cream,

Because to His eyes you are all,

His sons and daughters,

His creation's theme"

"Yes,

I know you well,

Your human heart,

And that is why I say again:

Love your brother and enemy as well,

For in heaven,

They are the same"

"Farewell, the time has come,

My journey takes me far away,

But before I leave you, I want to say:

If you would ever feel lonely

Or were looking for a guide,

Seek Him first, who loves you always,

He who loves you

And for you died"

May 5, 1968. Translated: November 5, 1996

Unknown to me at the time I wrote this poem, fifty years later it would be a source of consolation and a reminder that I was not alone and that yes, I was loved by Him who went to Calvary carrying my heavy cross.

4 MEDICAL SCHOOL AND TIME AS A RURAL DOCTOR

I was accepted to medical school in 1969 and for the following four years, my nose was mostly into the books, with little time (and less money) to do anything else. During school vacations, I would fly to my parents' home who were now living in Miami, and I would work with my father in a sugar mill, saving all earned money for next year's expenses. Even in this way, many times towards the end of the school year I was completely out of money and had to turn to my family for some assistance.

Medical school was demanding, but more demanding was their policy that any subject failed would automatically put you out of the school.   No makeover, no carryover. One strike and you're out. The reason they gave was that for every one of us admitted to the school, there were ten waiting for that spot and it was expensive to keep a failing student.

After graduation from medical school, I did a rotating internship at Hospital San Juan de Dios in San Jose and then, I opted to stay a year doing rural medicine as my token of appreciation for the opportunity they had given me.

The first six months of this year of rural medicine were spent in a very remote area accessible only by a small plane or by a train used by the banana plantations, with a car or two for cargo other than bananas including poultry, pigs, goats, and people as well. I was stationed at Guapiles, a tropical area in the Limon province where extensive areas of banana plantations were located.

The trip by plane took approximately forty minutes but it was extremely dangerous. On my trip there, the "pilot" was so drunk, he had to be helped out of the plane and a few days later, was killed in an accident. These accidents were the norm rather than the exception since the small planes had to cross high mountains through a small narrow pass, notorious for its high winds.

Of the trip to Guapiles itself, I remember arriving at Juan Santamaria airport in San Jose, and was taken to a side strip where a four-seat Piper plane was being prepped for take-off. The pilot was already in his seat as well as another person in the other front seat. I took one of the back seats, and the other one remained empty. I was excited because of my assignment and was eager to start practicing medicine.

It was a bumpy ride with many drops and side movements and a very loud noise that made conversation impossible. There was a heavy diesel smell and fumes inside the cabin. At the end of the trip, I remember having a headache, perhaps because of the noise, or even carbon monoxide poisoning.

The train ride took between eleven and fourteen hours, depending on the number of stops along the way. I only took one trip in each mode of transportation, one in by plane and one out by train and that was enough for me.

Costa Rica has a dual health care system, the Caja Costarricense de Seguro Social for those employed or who can afford it and the Public Health Care System, for the poorest citizens and unemployed. Everyone in Costa Rica has access to medical care. I was assigned to this latter category.

The health clinic in Guapiles cared for the indigents and the poorest of the population. The services provided at the clinic included general medicine, family medicine/pediatrics, and minor surgeries. We had a maternity ward with six beds and a delivery room that took care of mostly uncomplicated pregnancies, although on many occasions we were surprised by last-minute patients without any prenatal care at all.

We also provided emergency care for the many uninsured banana plantation workers that showed up at our doors at any time of day or night with signs of organophosphate poisoning, an insecticide used at that time, or injuries sustained during their labor.

I had a room to live in at the unit as my lodging. This was, for the most part, a 24/7 job, mostly due to the delivery of babies and the care of the frequently poisoned or injured workers who usually presented after they had finished their labor. In my six-month assignment there, I do not recall ever having a day off duty. There was also nowhere to go other than getting out of there by plane or train, which I did not want to do.

As the public health officer, I was also the coroner, a duty I was called to perform on several occasions. The one I recall best is the exhumation of a body from a ground tomb in a forest about five kilometers from town. I went prepared with surgical scrubs, gloves, masks, and plenty of perfume. The court personnel and laborers with their shovels all laughed at the way I was dressing for the occasion. However, once we got to the gravesite and they started to dig, I was the one laughing at seeing them turn green. I diligently found bullets fragments in the remains, which helped solve the case and clear an innocent person.

Because of the "education I had received", many times I was called to be the arbitrator in family issues and between neighbors. This was not something I was prepared for, nor expected nor enjoyed.

The second half of that year I spend in Buenos Aires, near the Pan American Highway toward Panama. This was a mobile unit, as well as the stationary clinic. Once a month I had consult days at the local health clinic. Besides the regular medical clinic, we also distributed food. When I arrived there, sixty families were coming to collect the bags of food, which consisted of cheese, large cans of oil, cans of butter, flour, and cans of milk, grains, etc.

After my third week there, I befriended the owner of the restaurant I frequently visited, and he inadvertently let me know that once a month there was an influx business for local bar owners and himself, where the recipients of the food bags would sell all the can goods or exchange them for liquor or beer.

Soon after this, I contacted some friends at the Peace Corps and the following month I had a complete team of them, teaching cooking, making sandals out of old tires, and building latrines. That month, instead of just handing out the bags, we requested everyone to first take the cooking class to better utilize what was given. Everyone had to use their products, which meant opening the cans and bags given, rendering them unmarketable. By the third month of doing this, only seventeen families were still coming and were very appreciative. Of course, I was questioned about the drop in the number of recipients of food bags but it was easily explained and confirmed. Many other clinics adopted the same procedures.

During the rest of the month, we went to different locations, mostly to indigenous and very remote places. One of these places in particular stands in my mind.

After a two-hour ride in a jeep, which carried the driver who was also the pharmacy dispenser, a nurse, myself, and all the medications, vaccinations, and antiparasitic we could muster, we had to cross a large river by canoe. Then, after a four to five-hour mule and horseback ride, we would arrive at a village high in the mountains. The locals always awaited us with the corresponding mode of transportation.

The canoes were hollowed-out trees with a rope attached to each end, one for each side of the river at an angle, with the downstream side further down about fifty to sixty yards from the launch area. Crossing this river always made us nervous because it was a fast, large river and the canoes rocked sideways, ready to roll over but never did. The natives always laughed at us while we were in the canoes, sensing our fright.

After arriving at the site, which was usually close to dusk, we stayed overnight in hammocks, in the central community building, and then clinic the following day. There were usually fifty to fifty-five people from all the surrounding areas.

There was only one person who spoke Spanish and she was our liaison to the natives. She also served as the nurse's aide while we were not there. She was always present during my consults to help me communicate with the locals.

Of course, as any government agency, I had to report our whereabouts and justify our expenditures as well as medications and supplies used, monthly. When I turned in the report, they didn't know this population even existed. That's how remote it was.

I was asked to document it on my next visit, by taking pictures and so I tried. I could only get the backside of most everyone scrambling for the bushes. I was trying to get pictures and a movie while they were setting up for us.

That was the last time we had any contact with them. The following visit was just an absolute waste of time, since nobody showed up. We found out that they believed we were taking their "spirits" with us in our cameras. We were not welcome there anymore.

The only good thing was that, on the previous visits we had vaccinated over 95% of the population, gave treatment for parasites to most of them, and left supplies for first aid and treatment of minor illnesses.

During that year, I had been keeping a diary that contained my experiences as a rural doctor and a few poems but this also has been lost in my move from Costa Rica.

During medical school, I tried to attend church at least on Sundays but sad to say, it was not as frequent as it should have been. During the year of rural medicine, I can't even recall if there was any church in Guapiles, and very rarely did I attend services while in Buenos Aires. How fast did I forget, the One who had brought me there!

5   Return to the USA as a Physician.

In 1975, I came back to the States and began a pediatric residency at Children's Hospital of Miami followed by a fellowship in Pediatric Hematology/Oncology at Emory University in Atlanta, Georgia, which I did not complete. All through this time, a certain restlessness began to grow within me and I did not know what it was. My church attendance was very poor, although I think I still had remnants of faith.

It was about this time I wrote a few other poems, including this one while "relaxing" in a Japanese garden that was located in the vicinity of Henrietta Egleston Pediatric Hospital in Atlanta, Georgia.

5.1   Fantasy. Poem

Fantasy

Last night,

After I got out of work,

I started walking,

To no particular place.

Suddenly, I woke up,

And found out,

That I was watching a pair of swans

RESCUED PILGRIM

In a little Japanese garden,

And that I was thinking,

How happy and lucky they were!

I saw them going,

Free to go where they pleased to go,

One beside the other,

Moving as if they were one.

They seemed to be talking to each other,

I presumed, about love,

And then,

You came to me, as a beautiful dream.

I saw you by my side,

Gentle as you are,

Saying words, I long to hear,

Perhaps,

The swan's same words.

After Emory University, I began to work as a pediatrician in a private practice setting in Clewiston, Fl, as well as working at the Health Department in Belle Glade, FL providing pediatric care to the poor. During this time, I rarely attended religious services or truly, thought much about God.

The pediatric practice was getting busier and busier and the workload correspondingly as well. I was well-liked and I liked working there.

All was well for several months but by year's end the restlessness was again rampant, and yet again, I thought of taking a different direction in life.

6   A SWITCH IN GEARS.

I went back to residency, this time in surgery, at Ohio Valley Medical Center, in Wheeling, WV where I met the love of my life, and shortly after, we were married. I started moonlighting in the Emergency Department of a small community hospital and I liked that line of work a lot.

My faith life was sporadic, mostly due to the hectic schedule in surgical residency and moonlighting. After marriage and while working in the Emergency Department, attendance to church got better, especially after our children were born and growing up.

This new specialty of Emergency Medicine was just in the beginning stages. I applied to sit for the Board examination by grandfathering into the specialty. I took the exams and became board certified in 1986. I practiced Emergency Medicine on a fulltime bases for 31 years, both in small hospitals and in trauma centers, where we also taught and mentored students and residents. I was also Medical Director for a paramedic program at a local community college.

The last 14 years of practice I spent as Medical Director of the department and Chief of Staff on two occasions at a rural Hospital where residents and students rotated in the Emergency Department. I retired in 2012 for family and health issues.

All along, I always felt a certain restlessness or emptiness despite apparently having it all. All material things that is, because even though we were attending church more regularly, it was not what I now see as true faith-filled. This restlessness I thought was a midlife crisis when I enrolled in and got an MBA degree at Wheeling Jesuit University which kept me occupied for a while, but of course, did not take that restlessness away.

But that is not to say that the Holy Spirit was far from me. Rather, it was me who was far from Him and once in a while He would try to wake me up by shaking me in my senses.

One of those occasions was at work. An E.R. nurse one morning was rather distraught and when I asked what was bothering her, she opened up to me in desperation and this poem just flowed from my mind as if a river going down a mountain. The real irony is that, twenty-five years later, this same poem was such a consolation and hope to me that I now have no doubts I had written it for myself, that long ago.

6.1 WORDS TO A FRIEND IN DESPAIR. POEM
Words to A Friend in Despair

Dear friend,

Sometimes we try too hard

To solve our problems,

To reach our goals,

Relying only on our strengths,

To find that alone, little we can.

It is when we hit bottom

And it seems to be the end,

That we look for wisdom,

In Him, who is our strength.

It is then we realize

That He is always there,

For us to turn to and lean on,

No matter what the problems,

No matter where we've been.

Hang in there friend!

Don't despair

And don't give up.

Let tomorrow be tomorrow,

Let things past, go,

Live for Him today and only,

Live for Him, who died for us.

I'll keep you in my prayers.

Martins Ferry, Ohio

September 11, 1992

The decades of the late '80s, '90s, and early 2000s was a busy time in my life. A demanding job and profession, in which I had to constantly be refreshed in an ever-changing specialty, raising a family of four and keeping an alpaca farm kept me busy. I tried my best, but in reality, I was absent for many of the family functions, not completely by choice, but none the less, absent.

If at home on Sundays, we attended church as a family but this was not always so. My wife would take the slack off in my absence and kept home and farm going as best she could.

I always felt something was missing in my life. But I was so absorbed in my busyness that I was completely deaf to my inner voice, although, once in a while, that still voice was loud enough for me to hear it. Retrospectively, the farther I drifted from God, the stronger and louder this voice became, but unrecognized by me as such at the time.

Many times, on my drives to or from work, different thoughts used to come to me out of the blue sky. The following poem was one of these thoughts that I had to pull over and jot down.

6.2 MEDITATION. POEM
Meditation

"It is in dying that we are born to Eternal Life"

St. Francis of Assisi, 12th century Monk.

How wonderful our God is! …Creator of everything and Master of all!

Today, while going to work, early in the morning

Of this beautiful Fall day, He has given us,

I was gently reminded of how much alike

Our lives are, to the seasons of the year.

In the spring of our lives, we are growing

Carefree and rapidly, perhaps with a guiding hand

That tends to us and nurtures our curiosity,

And plant the seed, which would grow

In our lives and bear much fruit much

Beyond their imagination.

RESCUED PILGRIM

Our summers are busy with the flowering and toiling

Of mundane affairs and hopefully

Also, with the nourishing of our desires

To fulfill the void within us,

A void that cannot be filled with things of this world.

During fall, nature comes to its splendor

With golden leaves and freshly scented air,

A full harvest and magnificent days and so are also,

The fall days of our lives,

The golden years of our existence,

The culmination of our seasonal presence on this earth,

The pinnacle of our youth.

In wintertime, life seems to come to an end.

The days are cold and dark and short,

The flowers of the meadow withers,

The lush vegetation languishes

And trees become barren, lifeless-like.

And when the glittering snow covers the fields

That once were vibrant with activities,

It now seems so peacefully empty

That we tend to forget

That life is just about to begin anew,

For without winter, spring cannot be.

As our winter approaches, we are reminiscent

Of springs gone by,

We cherish our summers and enjoy the fall days,

And we are also hopeful

That after our winter has passed

We awake to an Eternal New Life

In the presence of the Almighty God,

Creator of Heaven and Earth,

The Source of Life and Eternal Spring.

Fall 1996. Wheeling, WV

During the following few years, we were extremely busy with the construction of a house on our farm near Oglebay Park in Wheeling, WV, and this property was as pretty as the park itself. We started raising alpacas; and showed them and sold them all over the US. My wife had a boutique right on the premises, selling alpaca clothing and products, imported from Peru initially but later from the US, since it was then made here with our yarn and fiber.

We had the farm and boutique for about 13 years and if you know anything about farming, it is a very demanding job, 24/7, especially when you have a herd of 100 animals.

We got to be good and successful at it, but at a price. Most of the time, by day's end we were exhausted; church-going was not a priority anymore and social life was in a constant decline if it was not alpaca related.

By this time, I was the Medical Director of a rural hospital's Emergency Department, which gave me great flexibility to juggle both jobs. But being a physician requires a constant update of knowledge and frequent courses for certification and recertification and being the director required additional time for meetings both with Staff as well as administration. This also took a toll on the family and myself.

On one occasion, while visiting a son who was doing studies in Guanajuato, Mexico, I started to experience chest discomfort while walking uphill. I would stop walking, claiming to be taking pictures and the discomfort would stop. This came and went for a couple of hours. I knew exactly what was happening but did not want to alarm the family, so I "rested" the following day. The rest of the time there I was "fine", but as soon as we returned home, I called a cardiologist friend, and the following day I had a stent put in.

During the following few years, our family went through tremendous challenges, and eventually, my wife and I divorced after we moved to Florida. At this point in our lives, we were not attending church as a couple, and our prayer life was non-existent. I would rarely go to church by myself but this also stopped.

7   GOING INTO THE DESERT

During the time of separation and divorce, I felt an inner call to go into a self-imposed eremitic life in my place. You could say I had gone to the desert, to my "urban desert". This was a trailer I had bought right after we had moved to Florida and that I used as a carving/sculpture studio, where I did bird carvings and other works and painted them. We also used it as storage for things we didn't used regularly.

This structure sits in the middle of an acre of land with large and beautiful trees with an abundance of birds.

During this time of self-imposed seclusion seeking God, I only went out of the house for supplies, doctors' appointments, and to Sunday Mass. I adopted an ascetic lifestyle. I got rid of the TV, radio, newspaper, internet or any outside distractions, sold most of my valuables, and donated them to the poor. I was in an "urban cave", so to speak.

There was a lot of soul-searching, reflections, meditation, praying, studying the Scriptures, reading mystics, and even attending a few therapy sessions.

I read the Bible of course, and read/studied many books, among others: The Confessions by Saint Augustine; the Diary of Saint Faustina; Spiritual Combat by Lorenzo Scupoli; Ascent to Love by Ruth Burrows; The Ascent to Mount Carmel by John of the Cross; John of the Cross: Selected Writings, Editor Kieran Kavanaugh, O.C.D.; Fire Within by Thomas Dubay S.M.; Spiritual Childhood, the Spirituality of St. Therese of Lisieux by Vernon Johnson; The Story of a Soul; the autobiography of the Little Flower; Abandonment to God by Joel Guibert; works of St. Teresa of Avila including The way of Perfection, Meditation on the Song of Songs and The

Interior Castle; The Third Spiritual Alphabet by Francisco de Osuna; The
Practice of the Presence of God by Brother Lawrence of the Resurrection;
Sensing your hidden Presence: toward intimacy with God by Ignacio
Larranaga; The Spiritual Exercises of Saint Ignatius and my two favorites
and constant companions, Uniformity with God's Will by St. Alphonsus de
Liguori and The Imitation of Christ by Thomas A. Kempis.

Studying all these books meant a lot to my faith, however, now I know I
have received as many instructions and teachings while sitting quietly in the
adoration chapel or meditating at home, without reading a single word, by
just listening to God as He speaks into my soul's and heart's ears. We just
need to carefully be attentive to that still voice and discern Who is talking to
us and what He is telling us and of course, always look for that
confirmation of the Word of God as found in the Scriptures.

Initially, it was difficult for me to be completely still, quiet, without that
noisy world that I had retracted from, but imperceptibly, I became used to
it and now I love it. Difficult also is to quiet our mind, which when
secluded, becomes our main source of distraction. I am amazed at how
much beauty I had missed by not paying real attention before. God's voice
is indeed still, a whisper that we easily mute in the noisy world we live in,
with all its innumerable distractions.

I also began to listen to my inner "voice" and began to write, both prose
and poems. The prose is usually a meditation on certain passages from the
Scriptures or "thoughts" that comes during prayers. The poems are usually
spiritual, coming always from "within", spontaneously flowing while I never
really think about them. They are so spontaneous that I carry with me a
little notebook that as soon I start having these thoughts, I pull it out and
start writing or else I miss it. And this happens at times.

Most of the time these "thoughts" happen during meditation or
contemplation and some times in the middle of the night. They come out
fast, very fast, with just enough time to jot them down. I used to joke with
friends by saying that God could pick a different time to inspire me, not
just in the middle of the night.

As I began the encounter with my Almighty Father, thru His only
begotten Son, Jesus, by the presence of the Holy Spirit in my life, a change

began to happen.

A change imperceptible at first but real nonetheless. You see, up to this point in my life, even as I thought I was a "believer," I was very lukewarm at best.

To me, God was real but in a very distant place, high above, in heaven. I did believe in Jesus and the Holy Spirit but, did not have that close and personal relationship and the confidence to completely trust in Him in everything. I always needed to be in charge.

This transformation for me has been a slow process, by the realization that all events in my life were only leading me to it. Perhaps God, in His mercy and love for me. has chosen this way for my salvation. I always say "let thy will be done in me" and maybe this has been His will for me all along, since it did draw me closer to Himself. Certainly, the salvation of my soul had been in peril had He not in His great mercy intervened.

I began attending church every Sunday. Then I felt the need to go several times during the week, and eventually to everyday Mass. Slowly I felt drawn to spend few minutes in adoration of the Blessed Sacrament a few days a week. This grew to about an hour most days of the week, sometimes more than an hour in meditation and contemplation. Reading the Liturgy of the Hour has become part of my daily routine.

7.1   GUIDING SIGNS FOR MY CONVERSION.

I would like to share at this time a few entries from the notebook I have been keeping, in which I have written down "words" or "thoughts" that come to me during prayer time or at prayer group meetings and that I now see as guiding signs in the journey of my conversion.

- "My God, the thought that You are with me today makes everything endurable, and the hope to be with You in Heaven makes everything else meaningless."
- "I need your total surrender. Let go of everything"
- "Cast off your worries to Me."
- "I'll forgive all your sins and I'll fight all your battles but I require your unconditional yes to me."

- "Live in Me that I may live in you,"
- "Empty yourself of every earthly attachment, that's only when I can dwell fully in you. Remember that you are not of this world."
- "Learn from Me."
- "Be truly humble as I am humble, as Mary is humble."
- "You must have complete surrender to Me."
- "The poor is a gift through which many will be sanctified."
- "Mary, by her Fiat to the Holy Spirit made possible for the Divine to become fully human. We, by our unconditional yes to the Holy Spirit, make it possible for our humanity to become divine."
- "Live today to the fullest of your abilities, realizing it is a gift from God, that's why it is called "the present". It is also our only opportunity to mend our lives and mold it according to God's plans for us. God desires for us always what is good and best and so, we must learn to trust in His infinite wisdom, even as we don't yet see the "whys" of it. As we live in this way of complete trust in Him, there should be no worries or concerns about tomorrow, for it might never come for us, nor about the past, which is already gone and done with. We only have today, the present, now. Only God is always present in today, yesterday and forever. He is the same, unchanged and unchanging; an all-powerful yet all-loving and tender Father, who cares for us in our ever-changing present."
- "As a nation, you are doomed to disappear. No nation that has offended Me so much has ever survived. They all have been turned to rubble unless there has been complete repentance and returned to Me."
- "There is no doubt there is a battle raging on, but that battle belongs to Me. I'll fight that battle; you only need to trust in Me and give all of you to Me."
- "The battle is within and only love will conquer it. I am love and light and truth."
- "I have always loved you, even in your sinfulness and offenses against Me. For my love and mercy are greater than they

were. You are precious to Me since before you were created. Love and forgive yourself as I have loved you and forgiven you."

- "Cast all your worries to Me. Do not fear, for I am your God and I love you. Do not be deceived by this world. You belong to Me and I am not of this world. You are not of this world."

- "Martha, Martha, don't be a Martha. Only one thing is needed, only one thing is important for eternal life. Choose now and let everything else go."

- "The closer we get to our Lord, the bigger the battles are, and the more we have to trust in His love and mercy, for by ourselves, we stand no chance to succeed."

- "Let your hearts be not troubled nor you be afraid of anything, just put all your trust in My mercy. The battle is won by My blood."

- "Learn from Me. I became a little child for you. Now you have to be like a little child for you to have eternal life. You must trust like a little child trusts."

- Let your heart be My sanctuary, empty yourself of all that is not Me."

- "Let your life be a mirror of Mine."

- "There is no time wasted when you are near Me. I am time and I am space. I am light and I am truth. When you are close to Me, My love will permeate you, your fears will melt away and darkness cannot prevail."

- "I created you to be a living temple for Me to dwell in. I'll create in you a clean and pure heart if you but let Me and I will then dwell within you. It's up to you to call upon Me. I am standing at the door of your heart. I knock at it but only hear rumbles. If only you would open the door of your heart and let Me in, I'll dwell within you."

- "God calls us each by name. He has known us since the beginning of time, long before we were born. He allows us to wander about but always calls us back and takes us back with an even greater love than before we went astray. He desires for us to be the children He created us to be and for whom He revealed Himself and died, for our redemption and salvation."

- "Jesus' merciful heart is the narrow gate thru which we must pass to obtain the glory of heaven. He opens up wide, the gates of His merciful heart for us sinners, and pours out His mercy on us and brings us up to His glory, after we seek Him with a sorrowful and contrite heart."

- "God always dwells in our hearts. Our heart is His abode when we live a holy life, follow is commands, and love Him. When we sin, our hearts become His grave, for sin kills our love for God and therefore it becomes His grave."

- "If you want to be a saint, act like one"

- "Faith is to the soul what the senses, heart and brain are to the body, without them it is dead. Without faith, our soul is dead and headed to eternal damnation."

- "Who am I Lord, who dared to look at You while being weighed down by sin? Who are You Lord, that being the holiest of Holy, stoops down to my lowliness and lifts me from my filth and misery?"

- "Clean your house well for My coming. Your best gift to Me and the only I truly desire, is yourself. Your soul is My greatest treasure."

8 THE POWER OF FAITH AND THE HOLY SPIRIT

It was about this time I attended a Mass-healing service at our parish, intending to pray for a healing for my sister who has a serious and rare disease. During that particular week, I was having significant pain on my left knee which was close to the point of needing replacement. I was limping significantly and the knee was twice its normal size.

As the service progressed, my pain was intensifying, and I was by then unable to bear weight on the extremity. Somehow, when it was time to walk to the front of the church and have hands laid upon me, I did manage to do so. After imposition of hands, I was completely overtaken by this warm feeling of love. I could not even see anything except something like a white fog and felt as if floating. After I don't know how long, I was finally helped up and I walked back to the pew.

But then I noticed that I was standing on both legs and had no pain but reality didn't sink in until I got home and saw my knee looking completely normal and without pain. But this miraculous healing didn't stop there. I had been a Type 2 diabetic on oral medication for many years. On my next visit to my physician, it was noticed that my hemoglobin A1C was normal and I was taken off the medication. I have been off medication with normal tests for over two years now. Praise be to God for that. The knee has also been pain-free ever since. My sister has been stable or improving ever since. I think she has also been healed although she continues her medications. Her tests keep getting better.

It is during times in adoration that most of these poems flowed through my mind, sometimes so fast that I am unable to write them down completely, all at one time.

One such poem sums up my life's story, here it is:

8.1 RESTLESS HEART. POEM
Restless Heart

I can get no satisfaction

On this side of heaven,

Long have I tried,

Always coming out empty.

Although I have been blessed

With a clear mind and ease in studies,

A long and noble profession,

A comfortable life, family, health

And material goods,

I continually felt

A sense of emptiness

That I could not explain.

Now that I have nothing of what I once had,

I am more fulfilled than ever before,

But not yet complete.

I now look forward to the day

In which I finally leave my last earthly possession,

To be face to face

With the Love that truly fills my emptiness,

My God, my Lord, my Creator,

In whom is all my trust.

September 6, 2017

This poem was followed by a series of thoughts, mostly during prayer meetings or while reflecting on the Gospels. It was not until after Lent of 2018, another poem just flowed through my mind, certainly echoing the recent liturgical season. This is the poem:

8.2 THEN MAN ON THE CROSS. POEM
The Man on the Cross

He came down to pay, a debt He didn't owe,

To walk the road, just to show us the Way.

He came down to be Light, to those in the dark,

To be real Food and Drink, to those that thirst.

He came down to mend, as well as to split,

To breathe new Life, to those that are dead.

He came to pick grains, out of the weeds,

To call all the sheep, who'll hear His name.

He knows no stranger, that has ever been,

He calls brothers, and mother and sisters

All those who heed Him,

Both in Word and in deeds.

He loves without measure, and without cost,

Not only His kindred,

But all of us as well.

He calls us to be, His pierced hands and feet,

His heart full of love, His mercy to be.

He calls us above all to be,

The man on the cross,

To be truly free.

May 27, 2018

During the rest of 2018, most of the writings were prose in the form of meditations or thoughts. I would like to share with you two of those:

8.3   MEDITATION ON SANCTIFICATION AND PURGATORY

"God calls us to be Holy as He is Holy. But this is a task which is impossible to attain on our own accord. The good news is that when we ask Him for help to achieve this holiness, He will "shower" us with the graces we need. Many times in measures beyond our expectations and out of His infinite Love and Mercy for us, who are, of ourselves, undeserving of it.

We start to receive these graces in an ever-increasing measure as our trust and faith in Him grows and as our own will starts to conform to His will until, as His only Begotten Son's, they become the same.

We will all have to appear before the throne of God at the Final Judgment when "the sheep will be separated from the goat". Those found to be pure and worthy to be in His Holy presence will go into the eternal joy of praising and worshiping at the foot of His throne in the union of all His Holy Angels and Saints already there.

Those found not worthy to be in His presence yet, will have to go either to a place of purification, if their souls are found not to be completely expiated and pure or to a place of eternal damnation from which there is no escape, if their souls are stained with the shames of unrepented mortal sins.

Only Our Lord Jesus Christ and His Blessed Mother and yes, her most chaste spouse, St. Joseph, had been of the purity worthy to be in the presence of the Almighty God and Father without the need for any purification. The rest of us, including the saints who have gone before us, by the fall of our first parents, have inherited the stains of "original sin". And although perhaps venial, original sin gives us a propensity to commit graver sins deserving purification, not to mention the blotches caused by our sinfulness.

The place and time of this purification I believe starts right here on earth. It is available at the time of our birth and continues throughout our life. Only a few souls have achieved total purification of their souls while still of human flesh. Those are the Saints, declared by the church or otherwise, who have preceded us and are now in the presence and glory of our God and Creator, without further need for purification.

The graces required for our souls' purification are freely given to us by our Heavenly Father as He sees fit, according to our needs. God wants us to be holy and God does provide us with the means to attain it and this He does through His infinite mercy and love for us. Our souls can indeed be purified right here during this earthly life and thus avoid the need for further purification after our death. That is, we can avoid the purifying fires of purgatory altogether or at the least, reduce it to a minimum.

Most of the Saints recognized by the Church have modeled for us a sort of blueprint "road to holiness". They all have in common the following characteristics: a true and complete repentance and contrition for their sins; an unparalleled love for our Lord Jesus Christ, especially in the Eucharistic Presence and to His Blessed Mother. They all had a complete surrender of their own will to the will of God, in everything but particularly in the trials and sufferings they had gone through. They did everything just for the love of our Lord and Savior Jesus Christ, without ever seeking restitution or recognition either in the present life or the life to come. They fasted and prayed regularly including the rosary, and they all had a complete detachment from all things, both material and spiritual.

Those few souls that had been so purified during their life on earth had been bountifully rewarded by the All Omnipotent and Merciful God with the glory of His Presence, even before they have departed this life. At the hour of their death, they go directly to the everlasting joy of Paradise without the need for further purification afterward.

These are the Saints that through their lives had conformed their wills to the will of God the Father Almighty in everything but especially in times of trials and sufferings which are sure to come, offering them as a way of mystical union with the suffering of our Lord, for their salvation and the salvation of souls, for the conversion of sinners and the souls being purified in Purgatory. We can and should do likewise. This we can attain only with the help of God, which He is sure to provide us with all the graces needed. It is His expressed desire for us to be holy and it is His will for us since the creation of mankind.

He had sent to humanity many prophets to deliver His message with a rather poor response from our ancestors, until finally, he sent His Beloved Son to proclaim the Good News of Salvation and to shed His Precious Blood for our redemption.

Being God, He could have chosen any number of unimaginable ways to achieve that, yet He chose one of utter humility (God comes in human form, the babe Jesus); Jesus' total submission to the will of the Father in everything He did; immeasurable love and compassion towards everyone and everything created; total acceptance of the bitterness of trials and sufferings, most especially during His passion and death on the cross.

God is showing us that salvation of our souls is so precious to Him and that He loves us so much that He sent His only Son to shed His precious blood for us and to deliver that message of salvation personally, to each one of us through all ages.

Jesus, God's only son and God Himself shows us that our eternal salvation is worth dying even such a horrendous, harrowing, agonizing death as death on the cross and that, it is only thru the acceptance of that cross, whatever it happens to be in our life, that we can attain it. There is no salvation without acceptance of Jesus and the Cross. There is no sanctification without total acceptance and submission to the will of God.

Salvation is a gift from God Almighty, through the shedding of the precious blood of Jesus, His Son. We can't earn salvation. We can accept it or not, but we can't earn it. Sanctification, on the other hand, has to be earned. In other words, it needs our active participation in carrying out God's plan for us according to His will." September 16, 2018

8.4 "ON THE FOLLIES OF MAN"

"For man proposes but God disposes."

In today's gospel reading (Mt.24:42-51) we are told to be ready, to stay awake, because the Master will come in a day and hour not known. And somewhere else (1Thes. 5:2 and Rev 16:15) again we are reminded that He will come like a "thief in the night".

Since early in our lives we learn to make plans: we plan for college or some other trade or school, make plans for careers after college, vocations, weddings, honeymoons, jobs, businesses, etc. We place on ourselves all sorts of goals: career goals, family goals, financial goals, goals for retirement, and even "pre-need" funeral (goals) arrangements. But do we ever "plan" to meet God Almighty, our creator, and the Creator of the whole universe?

Whether we believe in God or not, at the end of our finite life we will NOT be here any longer, no matter what kind of plans we have had in place. All planning done will not be of any use to us, except maybe that of the funeral arrangements.

It would be indeed a miserable life if this was the only life there is, regardless of your conditions now. No matter how wealthy, healthy, happy, famous, or powerful we might be, there is an end to our existence on earth. We come from dust and to dust we shall return.

So, why would Jesus keep telling us to "be ready", "to stay awake," knowing that one day our lives would end? We don't have to prepare to die. That will happen whether we are prepared or not, whether we want it or not. There is absolutely no probability that we will not die. Then why does the Bible exhort us to be ready, to stay awake, to store treasures in heaven, not on earth, to be IN the world but NOT OF the world if this was our only life?

Is there something else we should be watchful for and guard? It's not the flesh we carry! Nor is it for our wealth or the possessions, degrees, titles, honorary positions, or status in society since ALL we have ever possessed stays behind when we die. So, what is it?

We can get a clue from the Bible. In the story of creation, in Genesis 1 we hear that God created man from dust and that He then BREATHED into him "life". I see here two distinct acts of God: first He created man from dust. Secondly, God then BREATHED into man "life". That is our 'non-physical life" if you would, that is our soul which is unique to us since the time of our conception and beyond our death.

In Genesis 3 we hear a reminder that we are dust and to dust we shall return. And that is absolutely true. But that refers only to our physical body, the flesh. What about the "other" part of us, the non-physical one, the soul? That part does not die! In those quotations from Genesis, nothing is said about the breath of life given to us as dying. That is what Jesus is concerned about here; to watch and care for our eternal, immortal soul.

We spend a great deal of time concerned about our physical wellbeing: careers, jobs, families, bank accounts, possessions, health, retirement, leisure, pleasures, etc., and prioritize our lives accordingly. All of these are just temporary stuff. No matter how wealthy, smart, famous, or powerful we might be, it all will end sooner or later. We can't take any of it with us when we die. We spend our entire lives behaving as if that is all there is, forgetting that man proposes and make all the plans he wants but it is God Who disposes.

There is nothing evil in planning for life in itself BUT this should always take a secondary priority. This life, no matter how long we should live, it's very, very short when compared to the eternity of the next life. Therefore, our main priority ought to be concerning where our soul (the non-physical part of us) will go after we return to dust.

Where will it go? At creation, God meant for us to be in Paradise but we all know what happened. However, we have another opportunity to get back in and a free will to choose where we want our souls to be. The stakes are high, so be ready. Stay awake, plan accordingly.

Don't believe in this? Just wait until you're dead to find out and it'll be too late then. As for me, I know the path I've chosen while there is still time! August 30, 2018

I spent most of the fall and winter of 2018 reading, going to church, and planning a cross country camping trip with my brother and sister in law, for the following spring.

While preparing for the trip, I increased the time spent in adoration at the chapel and many thoughts came to mind during these times. I have chosen to include some that I think are worthy to be shared.

8.5 RANDOM THOUGHTS

October 3, 2018. **Are we better than the Israelites** at the time Moses went up Mt. Horeb? Or during the Babylonian exile? We continue to ignore His voice and forget His commands and promises. We behave in the same way they did when God is not our top priority in every aspect of our lives. God must be our first love, above everything else--above our families, ourselves, even our wellbeing. God has to be the center of our thoughts, our will, and our hearts, for we were created with the sole purpose of knowing Him, adoring Him, and serving Him alone. That's what the Angels do constantly. That's what we are called to do here and now for that's what we'll be doing in eternity.

October 9, 2018. **While in adoration of the Blessed Sacrament.**

In the desert, during the exodus from Egypt, the Israelites complained about hunger, and God sent them daily manna from heaven, to sustain them in their journey to the promised land. When we say the Lord's prayer, we are likewise asking our Father, God, for that same food, our daily bread. In our exile journey to our heavenly Jerusalem, we need our daily heavenly manna, the bread from heaven as our Lord Jesus Christ said Himself to be {John 6:35}. During His last Passover meal with His disciples (Luke 22:15-20, Mark 14:22-25, Mathew 26: 17, 26-28) Jesus instituted the Eucharist, when, taking bread in His hands, blessed it and said "this is My body". Then taking a cup of wine, likewise, blessed it and said "this is My blood", the blood of the new covenant that will be shed for the salvation of many. He then gave it to His disciples and commanded them to do that in His remembrance. He also said that whoever eats His body and drinks His blood will have eternal life (John 6:51, 53-58)

So, when we are receiving the Eucharist, we are in reality, receiving the true body(flesh) and blood of our Lord Jesus, the true manna come down from heaven, that will transform us from sinners into Saints.

March 15, 2019. During Adoration. **Thinking about God's love**.

"God is love" and He loves us unconditionally, infinitely and freely. There is nothing we can do to increase God's love for us nor anything that can decrease it, because God's essence is love and it cannot be altered. God cannot NOT LOVE His creation, which He created precisely out of love. Because of that infinite love, God allows us the freedom to choose to reciprocate that love or not. To accept His love or not. Even in the absence of man's love for God, God's love for man is always present. Even when man thinks himself unlovable, God still loves him and He asks us to do the same.

March 22, 2019. During Adoration. **Meditating on the mercy of God.**

"No matter what our past has been or the gravity or number of our sins, God's love and mercy for us is much greater, as He clearly and emphatically told St. Faustina. I know and confess my great sinfulness but I also profess an unshakable trust in the mercy of God and His love for me and I submit myself completely to His will with hope in his Grace and to receive the strength necessary to overcome what is not pleasing to Him."

Another entry in my notebook I want to include here was written right after a period of contemplation while sitting on a bench by the Grotto at the Shrine of the Most Blessed Sacrament in Hanceville, AL. Here it is:

8.6 OH, HOW BLESSED I AM.

April 18, 2019. "Oh, how blessed I am! That after more than 70 years I have come to realize that my true love and fulfillment is in my Lord Jesus. That nothing else is of value or helpful to me, just a distraction and an allurement.

I said blessed, realizing how much God has and does love me and cared for me, even when I was not fully aware of it at that moment, even as I was running from Him. Now, I see His mighty hand holding me fast and guiding me back into His ways. I see His hand in my actions as well as in my writings, which I thought were a poetic inspiration geared to help someone, without really recognizing or acknowledging that it was, truly, a gift from Him."

The following meditation occurred to me while thinking about how the Holy Spirit transformed those in the Upper Room at Pentecost and how it transforms us when we are truly open to Its works:

8.7 TRANSFORMED BY THE HOLY SPIRIT. MEDITATION

"Do people recognize who you are? Do people that have known you for a long time, still see you as the same person they have always known?

Jesus walked this earth and lived among his friends and disciples for over three years and yet, after the resurrection, even those close to him didn't recognize him.

Have we died to our sins and resurrected to a life in the spirit? If so, people will notice something different about you. Some might even say "I didn't recognize you".

This happened to the Apostles when at Pentecost they were radically changed into new persons. From simple, ignorant fishermen and sinners to bold proclaimers of the resurrected Jesus and the Kingdom of God; from doubters and sometimes incredulous followers to champions of the truth and miracle workers; from cowards and deniers of the Master to firm pillars of the faith even unto death.

They were no longer the group of cowards hiding in the upper room for fear of the Jews. They were now different. If you would have known them before Pentecost, you would not recognize them now. There was something quite different in them. They had been filled with the Holy Spirit as promised and their lives would never be the same. What they previously denied, ran away from, hid from, they now fearlessly proclaimed. What they had previously marveled at, they now perform, all in the name of that which is above all names, Jesus. They were no longer the same persons and neither will be those so touched by the Holy Spirit.

Are you still the same person?

Ask the Holy Spirit to come and dwell within you. You will never be the same!

Come Holy Spirit, come into my life." April 26, 2019

9   CROSS COUNTRY CAMPING TRIP

This trip was to last until September as we began it in late April, 2019. It was during this time that the most amazing things happened to me and I was noticing them! The trip was to be a pilgrimage of sorts, stopping in most Basilicas and Cathedrals along the way.

I took a head start since my brother had some delays.

First, I stopped as already mentioned, in Hanceville, Alabama, at the Shrine of the Most Blessed Sacrament, a beautiful and most importantly, truly holy place. I attended Mass twice and my confession was heard.

After three days of a truly spiritual retreat and renewal, I continued on my way to our rendezvous point, Gulpha Campground in Hot Springs, Arkansas. My brother and sister in law were to arrive a few days later.

While there, I went to daily Mass at John the Baptist Catholic Church in Hot Springs, AR.

My first day there at the campground was spent exploring the surroundings and taking lots of pictures. The day after my arrival, I decided to get closer to nature and went for a hike up a mountain, to what is called "Goat Rock". The area was so beautiful and peaceful that I was overwhelmed by it and wrote in my journey entry:

9.1   EXPERIENCE AT GOAT ROCK, AR

"I went hiking by myself up to goat rock in Hot Springs, AR, in a rather chilly mid-morning on this 2nd day of May, 2019, at the beginning of a 5-month cross country camping trip which I call a "pilgrimage". I tried to absorb as much as possible the beauty that surrounded me and I became overwhelmed by such a peaceful and loving feeling that I knew I was not just in the presence of God's creation but of God Himself and I was moved to write: "Oh, how glorious it is to be in the presence of God and be immersed in His love! Words cannot describe it, nor would it be possible for it to be confined. It is not a sensation or a feeling, but a complete liberation from it. A burning desire in your heart to be completely and forever consumed by that love, and yet, I know that this is only but a taste of what it is to come. Why could I not remain so, forever, now? It makes me desire Heaven more and more, like a hungry man after tasting a heavenly morsel."

I was like in ecstasy for what it seemed a long time. Eventually, I made my way down the mountain, exhausted by the hike.

Later that evening, after resting awhile and eating supper, I was meditating and started to think about the earlier incident and how good my Heavenly Father had been to me and this poem sort of made its way into my heart and pen:

9.2 RESCUED. POEM
Rescued

I've been to places dark and dreary,

I've walked the road that leads nowhere,

I've played the games that life had dealt me,

I've tried my way and it only got me weary.

I've wandered far away

From the source of Light and Truth,

Stumbling along the way,

Wasting both time and youth.

RESCUED PILGRIM

I reached my life's goal,

And found myself an empty manhole.

Always searching for something to fill

That void within, that voice still.

Then I gazed upon the tree

That holds my Lord in agony,

And I came to realize,

To see and feel,

What in love for me He did

On that cross in Calvary.

Pierces my heart to see Him there,

Knowing He did it just for me,

To rescue me from the Gehenna,

To set me free from sin and its slavery.

And I'm ever thankful

And praises are always in my heart and lips,

For that selfless act of mercy,

That my Lord did just for me.

He died once, that is true,

But still upon the tree,

We find Him when we see

Injustice, hatred, blasphemy, and greed.

Take a stand,

Look at the tree,

Find my Lord from Calvary,

He will rescue you, just like me.

May 2, 2019

When my brother finally arrived, we took time to explore the city, went to the hot springs for which the area is famous for, and continue the planning of the next leg of the trip, which was San Antonio, TX. However, the weather was not cooperating due to an outbreak of tornadoes right on our proposed route, so we stayed a few extra days.

Amidst all this, one morning while still in my pajamas, I stepped out of the motorhome, and somehow, the door locked itself behind me. I have to admit, panic struck for just a minute, but then I walked to my brother's campsite asking him for "a key".

With a perplexing look, my sister in law asked me what the problem was, and I explained it to her. I asked her to bring a key to open my door. She said they didn't have a key to my motorhome but I insisted and so she tried with a random key and this miracle happened, the door successfully unlocked! Afterward, she tried to put that same key back into the lock again and it would not even fit!

With a break in the weather, we set sails toward San Antonio, and somehow, we missed all the terrible weather that was all around us.

While in San Antonio we visited, of course, the usual tourists and historic sites. However, most moving to us was being at Mass in the Mission San Jose Catholic Church, an active parish since its establishment in 1782.

After San Antonio, we continued to New Mexico, making stops in Carlsbad and caverns, Roswell, Las Cruces, going thru different "pueblos" and then setting up camp at the Pueblo de Cochiti, Lake and Reservation, which gave us access to both Santa Fe and Albuquerque.

One of the "pueblos" I visited on the way was the Isleta Pueblo that, although out of my route, I decided to visit for overnight parking at their casino. There was a Mission there, established in 1613, where the St. Augustine Church, an active parish since then, is located. Next to the church, there was a Grotto with different images of Our Lady but also a carving of an open hand of the Resurrected Jesus. This image shook me to the core because two years prior, I had awakened one night with that exact image in mind. I then carved it out of wood and painted it to look the same. I tried to find the origin and meaning of it but even the elders could only tell me that "it had been there a long time."

While in Pueblo de Cochiti, we did the "tourist thing" in both cities of Santa Fe and Albuquerque, did some hiking in the amazing Kasha-Katuwe Tent Rocks National Monument. We went to Mass at The Cathedral Basilica of St. Francis of Assisi in Santa Fe and visited the close by Loretto Chapel where the Miraculous Staircase is found and which is attributed to having been built by St. Joseph. I also went to El Santuario de Chimayo, about 25 miles north of Santa Fe, considered one of the most important pilgrimage sites, known as the Lourdes of America because of the numerous miraculous healings.

We then continued north to Colorado, toward Mesa Verde National Park, and stayed at their campground for several days, at about 8000 feet of altitude! During our first day there, we just laid around and were close to having high altitude sickness but by the following day, we were fine. We toured the archeological sites including the cliff dwellings as well as surrounding areas and cultural sites.

From there, we proceeded toward the Four Corners, where New

Mexico, Arizona, Utah, and Colorado meet, making stops at Monument Valley, Navajo reservations, Page and Lake Powell on our way to Bryce Canyon, where we spent over two weeks. This place is gorgeous, making us reflect on why, at creation, God was pleased with His work.

It was in one of my hikes around the rim of Bryce Canyon, that I sat down on a fallen log just to observe the beautiful scenery and somehow my mind drifted into a deep contemplation which then let into the following meditation:

9.3 MEDITATION ON DEATH

Is life an illusion ended at death? Is that the reason so many fear death?

Or is death a radical, inevitable, transforming event in the journey of life to everlasting life?

Jesus many times said we should learn from Him. He also said He came from the Father to do the Father's will, that He and the Father were one and that He would return to the Father, as He did after his passion, death, and resurrection.

If we really believe we have been created by God in His likeness and image (out of His infinite love) and that God (Father, Son, and Holy Spirit) is an infinite, indescribable, inexhaustible, all-consuming Love, then we can be assured that, in essence, we are also love, which must return to its source, God Himself.

So then, death is for us a transforming event that liberates our true likeness of God (our true self) to return to its source.

The circle of life (the continuing cycle of life, death, life) in which we are dust and to dust we shall return, can also be applied to we come from God (created by His love) and to God we shall return. That is our destiny, our "karma" so to speak and it is the best reason to live a life worthy to deserve it.

We shall see death then, not as a terminal event but as a transforming one, a liberating event that allows our true God-given self to return (reunite) to its source forevermore.

July 2, 2019.

10 ENDING THE TRIP

We planned to continue up to Grand Teton National Park, then through Yellowstone Park and then toward the Badlands of South Dakota, crossing to Canada, returning via Niagara Falls and down the East coast. That's what we had planned, but God had a different plan for us and we listened.

My brother's truck, which pulled his fifth wheel, was giving him some trouble and started to emit dark smoke. He tried to get a diesel mechanic around the Bryce Canyon area but nobody would even look at it. After praying about it, we decided to cut the trip short and return straight home.

As it turned out, the area in which we had planned on staying, near the Grand Teton National Park, had a large fire compromising the area, and the following week they had flash floods and flooding. If the truck had been working properly, we would have been casualties because that was precisely the area and time we would have been camping there.

On our way back, there were few glitches with the truck but eventually, we got home safely. The total duration of the trip was over three and a half months and we traveled close to 20,000 miles.

11   RETURNING HOME...CLOSER TO GOD

After unpacking the motorhome and resting from the trip, I went back to my usual routine of daily Mass, Adoration, reading, and feeding the homeless on Sundays. Although I had continued praying and meditating during the trip, there was a dry period right after the episode in Goat Rock. There was not much writing for the next couple of weeks. However, this soon changed.

In mid-August, I woke up one night at three in the morning and started to write the following:

11.1 CHRIST IN THE EUCHARIST. MEDITATION

"To see Christ present in His Eucharistic form, we have to look with the eyes of our soul, that is, with faith. When we look at the Eucharist with human eyes, we see only a tiny piece of white wafer and as much we try to rationalize, our brains only register a tiny piece of bread. To see the Real Presence of Jesus in the consecrated host, we have to look with the eyes of our soul, that is, in faith. Then, the real meaning of the eucharistic Body, Blood, Soul and Divinity of our Lord is made manifest, and the clearer our soul's vision is, the clearer we will see the true meaning of the Eucharist. That is, the stronger our faith, the better we will be able to grasp the reality of Jesus' presence. Jesus instituted the Eucharist for the church militant, as His gift for us, and as His promise to be always with us.

When we are in adoration of the Blessed Sacrament, we are

looking at Jesus himself. We are in His presence, albeit in a veiled form, but He is there. He is listening to us, talking to us, and with us. We just have to be attentive to His voice and listen with our soul's ears, and even sometimes with our physical ears as well. Sometimes we don't recognize Him but He is there, His graces are being poured out to us, His love is there, just waiting for us to be desirous of them and fully receptive to them.

The same Christ that walked on earth, cured the sick, expelled demons, resurrected the dead and forgave sinners is present in the Eucharist, still willing and waiting to heal the sick, expel demons, resurrect the dead and forgive sinners. We have only to approach Him, implore Him with faith and trust and believe when He says that He will be with us until the end of time, that whoever believes in Him will never die."

One day, while reflecting on my own life's experiences, suddenly this poem gushed out of me.

11.2 NOTHING. POEM
Nothing

We were created,

Out of no things.

And to nothing,

We are daily returning.

When we were born,

We brought no things with us.

And when we die,

We'll take no things as well.

No thing can buy us true love.

No thing can give us health.

No thing can bring us peace and joy.

No thing can give us lasting wealth.

No thing survives the rust, the moth, the thieves.

No thing endures the time.

No thing will save our souls.

No thing will bring us Christ.

No thing will give us Life.

So then…

Why always seek for things,

If no thing can give us nothing?

We should seek instead

The unseen treasure,

Stored in Heaven above.

Where neither rust nor moth or thieves

Can ever get or touch.

Treasures that would bring

True love, peace, and joy.

A lasting wealth

That will save our souls.

A treasure that's in God our Lord.

The source of Love,

Of Light,

Of everlasting Life.

October 24, 2019

The following week I woke up at two in the morning with this idea of "being a bridge" and this is how this poem just flowed through my mind:

11.3 THE BRIDGE. POEM
The Bridge

When you can't be a lighthouse for the sea,

Or a shining star that takes you far,

You can simply be

A humble bridge.

When you extend your hand to those in need,

When you greet and smile

Those you meet,

You simply are being

RESCUED PILGRIM

A humble bridge.

When you cry with those

Who mourn and weep,

And rejoice with those

Who are merry and cheerful;

When you give hope to those that despair

And call on those who seem not to care,

You simply are being

A humble bridge.

And when you're thinking about

Why being a bridge,

Just think about

The crucified Jesus on that ridge.

He was the bridge

Between heaven and earth.

He was God, yet human by birth.

He was the bridge

Between life and death.

He was the bridge

To save those on earth.

October 29, 2019

After this poem, I began to notice that at times it was very difficult for me to be able to pray for any length of time without significant mental disruptions and distractions. It was a struggle just to pray or keep my mind from flying everywhere. It lasted for more than a month this time although I tried to keep my daily routine and even this was a struggle. One morning during prayers (lauds) I turned back toward the church's stained-glass window depicting the Stations of the Cross after being alerted by another person, as the sun was shining brightly thru the one panel and I wrote this:

11.4 GOD'S RESPLENDENT LIGHT. POEM
God's Resplendent Light

Today, at morning prayer time,

We were given a glimpse

Of what Sts. Peter, James and John

Experienced at Mount Tabor.

A ray of celestial light

Shone thru the front glass window,

Right thru the panel of Jesus carrying the cross

And it transformed it into a magnificent scene

Of pure golden glow,

As these words were being read;

"Father all-powerful,

Let your radiance dawn in our lives,

That we may walk in the light of your law

With you as our leader."

Thank you, Lord, for this beautiful moment,

That some may think a coincidence,

But I know that for You it was not.

Let your radiance always shine on us

To guide us in the darkness of these times.

November 7, 2019

Right after this dry period, I began to have a profound longing for the Lord. My time in adoration, alone in the chapel, became now hours at a time and for me, time stood still, until the church's bell would ring time after time or they would let me know that they were closing the chapel for the day. It was during one of these days I wrote the following poem:

11.5 THE LONGING. POEM
The Longing

As a lover longs for his beloved

And as the ocean's waves seek its shores,

So my soul longs for You, Oh Lord.

For You I wait

In hopeful anticipation.

With distance,

RESCUED PILGRIM

A lover's love would increase

And the waves of the ocean grow bigger,

So, our waiting for Your coming Oh Lord,

Is filled with joyful preparations

And a watchful attitude.

We long for You, Lord,

For so You have created us,

That without You we wander aimlessly

And find no solace

In anything but You.

It is You, Lord,

Who first longed for us,

When You drew us to yourself

In the manger at Bethlehem,

Or when calling your disciples

Out of the fishing nets,

Taxing post or daily lives.

Or when You went preaching

And teaching the Good News of salvation.

But most of all when at Calvary,

Dying on the cross You said: I thirst.

Lord, You long for the souls

That in love You've created,

That through sin has turned from You;

But with great mercy and just judgment

You call to repentance and change.

We wait for Your coming

As You've promised You would do

And we pray for Your Graces

That You find us worthy of You.

December 10, 2019

Two days later, again while doing meditation and contemplation, unexpectedly this poem started to develop. My meditation was completely unrelated to the subject matter of the poem.

11.6 THE ARCHITECT. POEM
The Architect

Rebuild a dwelling place,

Proper for a humble king,

Where the afflicted, the poor, and the lonely

can find solace,

Where peace and love are akin.

You will need to tear down

The walls built by your pains,

And for this, I offered my crown,

Worn at the cross for your gain.

You will have to reinforce

your foundation on the Rock,

And be watchful of your course,

And be ready to be mocked.

You must change the paradigm

Of your innermost life and taste,

Then I'll make My dwelling place

In your heart, turned from stone to flesh.

This might look a daunting task,

Too deep, too long, too sore

to do alone,

But remember, always ask,

For My Presence in your soul.

This task will be much easier

and the burden will be light,

When you take Me as your guide

To rebuild your house again.

And when you're finished with this temple

And you meet Me at the door,

You will find that in your toiling

I was there as your Lord.

December 12, 2019

With the Christmas season and its busyness, I did not write much, although I kept my same routine. Right after the New Year, I woke up one night close to dawn with a song in my mind with words I didn't understand, only the word "ruah" was clear, which I had to look up, since it was new to me. It turned out to be a word of Hebrew origin, meaning spirit or breath of life and that's how this poem originated.

11.7 RUAH. POEM
Ruah

Let the Fire burn in your hearts

And transform you from within,

Like the pilgrims from Emmaus,

Like those in the upper room.

You will then see, in a different light,

And will sing, to a different tune.

You will walk the road upright,

And will shine, like the sun at noon.

You will boldly proclaim

The good news of salvation,

And with your lives and voices acclaim,

Jesus Christ, our redemption.

Like the apostles, you will be

Bold proclaimers of the Truth.

And like them, you'll change to be,

Courageous affirmers of the "crux".

But for this tenuous flame to come alive,

One must care not to smolder it

With the clingings of this world,

And it must be fanned into a fire

By the Spirit and the Word.

This breath of life, given to us

By our God and Creator,

With care, love, and perseverance,

Will bring about much fruits

And a plentiful harvest

For the kingdom of God.

We must always call upon our God,

Father, Son, and Holy Spirit,

To be present in our souls.

And we'll know of His presence

By the transformation

In the way we live our lives.

If we are not transformed,

We have not met our Lord,

Or have chosen not to change,

For it is impossible to meet Him

And continue to be the same.

January 5, 2020

The next poem had its origin right from the Saints. As it happened, on that day there was at church a brief talk about a group of Saint's relics being shown at the parish center. There was a total of 165 relics each with a brief description. Many of the Saints I knew about, many more I didn't.

As I went through all the tables, reading and meditating on them, I began to have an "urge" you might call it, to start writing. I sat down on a bench outside the hall and within a couple of minutes that "urge" was gone, but not before I had written this.

11.8 To be a Saint. Poem
To Be A Saint

To be a Saint, It's a choice.

A choice we have to make

Every second of every minute of every day.

A choice to be loving and caring,

Selfless in everything and to everyone.

To be poor, in spirit and flesh,

To be last and the least, here on earth.

To seek nothing, but Him on the cross.

To do God's will in all our quests.

To die to ourselves

And live,

Just to praise and to serve Him alone.

To be a Saint,

You need to love silence

and be able to be alone with God.

To hear His voice deep in your heart,

And change your mortality

By dying to the world.

To be a Saint,

It's a call we must answer,

Each one on its own.

By a different route and in a different way,

For we are all called to be holy,

It's a matter of choice.

God created us to be holy

And gave us a free will,

So we can choose to be His, wholly.

Or choose not to be.

To be a Saint,

It's to be part of the church,

Christ's mystical body.

It's to have a great love for His Holy Mother

And to His Eucharistic Presence as well.

It's to have perfect union

With the triune God,

Creator, Transformer, and Lover of our soul.

February 4, 2020

How comforting and encouraging has been to me reading the lives of Saul of Tarsus, Augustine of Hippo, and Ignatius of Loyola. Or reflecting on Mary, the woman from Magdala, or the Samaritan woman at Jacob's well or the tax collector at the back of the church. I can see myself in them before their encounter with our Lord and I pray and hope for the grace to have been transformed by that encounter also and so, I put all my trust in Jesus.

The following week, while meditating, at Valentine's day, it occurred to me what would I give God on that day if I could. This was my answer:

11.9 IN LOVE WITH LOVE. POEM
In Love with Love

What can I give?

To the love of my love,

Who has given, all in this life.

Who has, so much forgiven

And has everything,

In the palm of His hand.

What can I give?

Since love can only be repaid in kind,

And everything we receive

Is His, I remind.

RESCUED PILGRIM

If I give Him all my love and my life,

I'm just returning what it was not mine.

Same with possessions,

Honors, talents, and time.

What can I give?

To the love of my life,

Who humbled Himself to be just a babe.

Who bore our flesh, our cross, our death.

Who gave us new life by His passion and death.

Who went up to Heavens to prepare us a place.

What can I give in return then?

Is there anything I could give?

To the One who in all is,

From Whom all be,

And through Whom all is,

That is not already His?

There is only one thing

I could possibly give,

And that is myself.

That my will be like His

And my love be His love.

February 14, 2020

Beginning the liturgical season of Lent starts with a stern reminder of our mortality on Ash Wednesday and all the readings for the season are likewise oriented to guide us to repentance and change of our sinful ways. While I was meditating on a particular reading of the Old Testament, this poem came to my mind:

11.10 IN SACKCLOTH AND ASHES. POEM
In Sackcloth and Ashes

The people of Nineveh, from great to small

Paid heed to the prophet and declared a fast.

They didn't delay to acknowledge their wrongs,

They dressed in sack clothes and put on the ashes.

They came to grips with all their faults

And prayed to God to spare their own.

And God in His mercy after seeing such faith,

Spared the city from the doom they deserved.

This is a good lesson for us to learn from,

For we are not better, in our own ways.

In this Lenten season,

RESCUED PILGRIM

Of praying, fasting, and almsgiving,

Let's change our ways

And pray to our God to spare us as well.

And as we clothe ourselves in sack clothes

and put on the ashes

Let's have true repentance, and change.

Let the sack clothes and ashes

Be rather in our hearts and souls.

So our heavenly Father would have compassion

And spare us all, from being lost.

The people of Sodom and Gomorrah

Did not heed to the words of the prophet.

Their sins were as scarlet and crimson,

They refused and resisted repentance,

And the sword consumed them all.

The scriptures are clear,

We have been warned.

We choose either life by repentance

Or death by our pride not to obey.

March 1, 2020

Every Friday of Lent, our church has Exposition of the Blessed Sacrament right after morning Mass with Benediction late afternoon. It was on the first Friday of Lent while I was in contemplation and while staring at the crucifix and the Blessed Sacrament in the monstrance, that I was overtaken by this loving feeling and suddenly found myself scribbling this poem as fast I could in order not to miss a word:

11.11 THE LOVE OF JESUS. POEM
The Love of Jesus

Looking at Jesus

In the most Holy Sacrament at the Altar

And at Jesus on the cross,

I see **love**,

An indescribable, immeasurable, everlasting love.

That same love,

Which moved Almighty God to creation

Of the universe and mankind.

That same love,

Shown throughout salvation history,

And that moved God to be incarnate

In the virginal womb of Mary.

That same love,

RESCUED PILGRIM

That carried our Lord Jesus Christ

During his earthly life,

And through His Passion, Death, and Resurrection.

That love that is present in every tabernacle of the world.

That same love,

That has forgiven me so many times,

And that, despite my wretchedness,

Keeps calling me back,

And keeps loving me,

As if I never nailed Him to the cross.

That same love,

He asks me to have toward others,

Even to the point of suffering as He did for me.

That same love,

Which He has for the Father,

And asks me to have for Him too.

March 6, 2020. at Adoration.

12 GOD NEVER GIVES UP ON US

Perhaps it is my faith that makes me see the guiding, loving hand of God the Father, carefully and imperceptibly, bringing me back from a path that was leading me to be eternally far from Him, forever lost in damnation. As the Apostle Peter says "He has won you for Himself, and you must proclaim what He has done for you: He has called you out of darkness into His wonderful light" and so, I'm trying to do just that.

Our God is indeed merciful and loving. A loving Father that welcomes us back and rejoices upon our return. Praised be always our God and Creator for He has called us out of darkness into His wonderful light.

It is indeed comforting to hear our Lord Jesus' words that He came to heal the sick since the healthy do not need a physician. Our souls had been sick with our sinfulness and yes, we need our mighty Healer. I can only make mine the words of St. Augustine, "And now, Lord, these things are passed by, and time hath assuaged my wounds" and I add; and You have rescued me.

I was once reflecting on the "Parable of the Prodigal Son" and wrote the following which I think now appropriate to include:

12.1 PRODIGAL SON MEDITATION
Lk 15:11-32

"I think that in this parable Jesus is telling us much more than what most of us take out of it. We look at the obvious, that is, the younger son who squanders the share of "his" inheritance in a life of dissipation which eventually came to an end when his fortune ran out. Then he came to his senses, repents and goes back to his father who goes and meets him while he is still on his way.

We also might look at the older son, who had always been at the father's side and resents his father's welcoming of his youngest son.

Or we could also look at the third protagonist in this parable, the father, who loves both sons in great measure.

I see this parable as encompassing our relational attitude to God and shows us the spectrum of it, from our selfishness and sinfulness to our ignorance and pride and details the steadfast love of our heavenly Father towards us, regardless and despite us.

His love for us is unchangeable, infinite, and irrevocable! God always loves us and always desires to be loved by us but doesn't need our love. We, on the other hand, need to be loved and need to love.

The younger son in this parable selfishly demanded his share of what would be his inheritance and with this, he is wishing his father's death. He then turns his back and leaves him, seeking his pleasures and his own will.

We do the same thing when we put anything at a higher priority than God or that which leads us to God, whether it be money, fame, pleasures, relations, success, or whatever else, even our good acts of charity. Or when we misuse or waste our gifts and talents freely given us by our Father.

The older son never really saw himself as a son but rather as a servant of his father. He didn't appreciate nor recognize himself as an heir of the father and was resentful of the father's generosity and love toward his brother whom he also denied.

We can also be like the older son when we take for granted God's love for us; when we fail to recognize that our very life is a gift freely given; when we act as if we own whatever is that we may have or when we desire that which we do not possess; or worse yet, when we wish to possess what someone else has.

115

We also act as the older son when we have an attitude of righteousness or jealousy toward others we see as unworthy of the gifts or merits they receive.

Many times, men (all of us), fluctuate between these two extremes until, as the younger son, we realize that our place is in the Father's house and have a change of heart so to speak, recognizing our own mistakes, acknowledging the harm done, seeking to repair it and asking for pardon.

The father, in all of this, has remained with an unchanged love, unaffected by the great offense intended by the younger son. As soon as the sinner had a repentant heart and took the first steps toward him, he rushed to meet him on his way home, showered him with the best gifts and called for rejoicing in his house. This is how our heavenly Father welcomes us, sinners, upon our repentance, with open arms and rejoicing in heaven.

The Father as well, went out to call his older son and reminded him that indeed he was his heir and so showed him His love also.

13 CLOSING THOUGHTS AND PRAYERS

I was meditating the other day on the constant struggles we face and that those struggles and temptations can serve as a means for growth in holiness, and that as long as we live, they'll be always present and these words came to me:

13.1 THE BATTLE WITHIN
The Battle Within

A battle rages within us.

The battle between the loftiness of our soul

that seeks its creator,

and the corruptness of the flesh,

that seeks its pleasures and comforts.

My soul longs to do God's will,

but my nature urges me

to this created and sensual world.

I know the things eternal,

yet I am inclined to do

what is temporal.

I am born from above,

Yet I trample in the dust.

Alone, we are helpless against the powers that seeks to keep us grounded on this beautiful creation, overlooking its Creator and leading us into a path of darkness. Only by relying and trusting in the higher power of God can we overcome our innate inclinations and those exerted on us by the adversary ruler of this world. Only with total confidence and reliance on the grace of God through the Holy Spirit are we able to overcome ourselves and the world. May 5, 2020

We fail and fall many times but we can and should, always, return to the waiting open arms of our Abba, Daddy, who is always there for us, waiting for our repentance and change of heart. "What father would give his son a snake when he asks for a fish?" So much more our heavenly Father will give to us, adopted sons and daughters by virtue of our Lord Jesus Christ, those things we, in faith, ask of Him, if they are for our spiritual benefit and salvation or that of those for whom we ask.

Our heavenly Father knows better than we do what is beneficial for us. We only have a biased short-term vision of ourselves. He has the big picture before Him, since the beginning of our existence, since the beginning of time.

I have seen this firsthand. My life has taken many twists and turns along my journey. Many had been the wrong turn, usually while following my desires and pleasures and my own will. But by His infinite love and mercy, somehow, they have turned out to be for the benefit of my soul's salvation, which ultimately, as a Christian believer, is the final destination of this earthly pilgrimage.

I honestly think that many of these twists and turns have been God's will for me, since they have led me back to Himself. He has allowed many of the "evils" in my life to happen, to teach me the lesson that, away from Him I am lost and helpless and that my true place is in His presence. He had given me plenty of opportunities and yet I was blind, deaf, and close to death. Perhaps this was the only way I would have returned to Him. As the tax collector in the parable in Luke 18:9-14 I pray, "Lord Jesus Christ, son of the living God, have mercy on me a sinner".

How are the last few chapters of this poem of my life going to unfold? Only the Author of the poem can answer that question. My only resolution toward that is: "let Thy will be done in me and through me." I have no plans or desires for my life other than trying to do God's will in everything, whatever that may be, and to allow to be transformed and consumed by His love. I have never been more joyful or peaceful since I made that resolution. I have no worries or concerns at all, about anything, whether it be health, financial, life, or death even in the face of this pandemic. Not that I am healthy nor wealthy, but because I am learning to turn all into the hands of Him who has all in His hands. Lord Jesus, I trust in you and I love you above all things!

St. Thomas Aquinas, among his many writings, wrote the following prayer which we are wise to take to heart:

> "Oh, merciful God, grant that I may ever perfectly do Your will in all things. Let it be my desire to work only for Your honor and glory. Let me rejoice in nothing but what leads to You, nor grieve for anything that leads away from You. May all passing things be as nothing to me and may all that is Yours be dear to me and You my God, be dear above them all. May all joy be meaningless without You and may I desire nothing apart from You. May all labor and toil delight me when it is from You.
>
> Make me, Oh Lord, obedient without complaint, poor without regret, patient without murmur, humble without pretense, joyous without frivolity, and thankful without disguise.
>
> Give me, Oh Lord, an ever-watchful heart, which nothing can ever lure away from You; a noble heart which no unworthy affection can draw down to earth; an upright heart that no evil can tempt aside; an unconquerable heart which no tribulation can

crush; a free heart which no perverted affection can claim for its own.

Bestow in me, Oh God, understanding to know You, diligence to seek You, and wisdom to find You; a life which may please You and a hope which may embrace You, at the last."

I started the book with a prayer I composed and say every morning. I'll finish likewise by sharing another of my prayers.

O my God, I beseech You, give me always a desire to seek You; wisdom to recognize You; courage to follow You, and the love to imitate You in all I do. At the hour of my death, let me be surrounded by a host of Holy Angels and Saints; by my Guardian Angel; by the Archangels Michael, Gabriel, and Raphael; by St. Therese of Lisieux, St. Augustine, St. Faustina, St. Charbel, and St. Padre Pio and let me take my last breath in my heavenly mother Mary's arms, listening to her loving lullaby next to my Jesus, under the watchful eye of St. Joseph. Amen

Made in the USA
Columbia, SC
24 December 2020

27760791R00076